Just-In-Time
Purchasing

Just-In-Time Purchasing

A. Ansari
B. Modarress

The Free Press
A Division of Macmillan, Inc.
NEW YORK

Collier Macmillan Publishers
LONDON

Copyright © 1990 by The Free Press
A Division of Macmillan, Inc.

The Free Press
A Division of Macmillan, Inc.
866 Third Avenue, New York, N. Y. 10022

Collier Macmillan Canada, Inc.

Printed in the United States of America

printing number

1   2   3   4   5   6   7   8   9   10

Library of Congress Cataloging-in-Publication Data

Ansari, Abdolhossein.
    Just-in-time purchasing / A. Ansari, B. Modarress.
        p.   cm.
    ISBN 0–02–900971–5
    1. Just-in-time systems.   2. Industrial procurement.
    I. Modarress, B.   II. Title
    TS156.A56   1990
    658.5′6—dc20   89–25659
                                                             CIP

To our son
Alexander

Contents

Preface

How many articles or books have you seen recently on Japanese manufacturing techniques, namely just-in-time (JIT)? How many regional, national, or international conferences have you attended in the past few years where you heard stories about how well the Japanese have been served by JIT? If you are involved in the field of materials management, your answer is probably "a lot." Even if you are only indirectly involved, the response may still be "a lot."

The articles and conferences tell the story of how the JIT manufacturing system has been implemented in Japan, and why the Japanese are more successful at producing a high level of product quality and a higher rate of productivity than their American counterparts. Many factors have contributed substantially to Japan's high quality and productivity, but the focus on JIT has stirred the interest of American management. Today, a growing number of U.S. manufacturing firms (both small and large) are adopting the JIT manufacturing system in order to improve their product quality and increase productivity.

The implementation of the JIT system has significantly altered the way many companies plan and control their in-house production facilities. This same JIT manufacturing system has altered the relationship between buyers and suppliers as well. As these changes occur, JIT purchasing becomes a necessary and important factor in a successful JIT manufacturing system.

Unfortunately for those of us interested in developing JIT purchasing systems, the articles and seminars have given only a superficial understanding of JIT purchasing. The purpose of this book is to describe in depth the successful implementation of JIT purchasing by many U.S. manufacturing firms, and the accompanying problems and benefits. These detailed accounts will explore the critical success factors identified by purchasing managers, factors that may assist other firms considering JIT purchasing implementation.

WHY ADOPT JIT PURCHASING?

If JIT has worked so well for the Japanese, will it also work in the United States? Is JIT the key to increasing product quality and productivity?

The first reaction of many American managers to pursuing JIT purchasing practices is negative. They say the practices have worked well for the Japanese because Japan is an island with limited industrial land mass, certainly small in relation to the vast distances between U.S. industrial centers. This reaction reveals a limited understanding of JIT.

American manuacturers should at least examine the JIT purchasing perspective and consider unlearning years of knowledge and experience with traditional purchasing practices. Many think of JIT practices simply as purchases in small lot sizes. JIT purchasing is far more than that. It also includes supplier selection and evaluation, bidding practices, incoming inspection procedures, inbound freight responsibility, paperwork reduction, value analysis practices, and packaging aspects. When all these activities are considered together, the purchasing department can add value to the product and become a "quality and productivity center" for the firm. Such a broadened view of the purchasing concept should promote a closer look at JIT purchasing.

In the past few years, many U.S. manufacturers—such as General Motors, Ford, Hewlett-Packard, Nissan, Xerox, Honda, Sony, Kawasaki, IBM, and John Deere and Company, to name a few—have substantially improved their product quality and productivity by adopting JIT manufacturing strategies. Our survey of current practices in JIT purchasing and statistical quality control (SQC) among these and other manufacturers suggests some compelling reasons for adopting the new purchasing approach.

Implementing JIT purchasing has produced dramatic economic improvement. At Hewlett-Packard, Greeley Division, for example, inventory turnover has nearly tripled; scrap cost has declined from 10 percent to 1 percent; and delivery lead time has been reduced from 90 to 64 days. JIT practices at the Kawasaki Lincoln Plant resulted in an increase in total sales from $51,536 million to $74,430 million and a decrease in manufacturing costs from $15,167 million to $12,600 million from 1980 to 1985. These JIT purchasing results are a powerful motivator for change.

Even greater benefits are envisioned at companies like Hewlett-Packard when the system is fully developed (within the next few years). At Hewlett-Packard, inventory turnover is expected to improve approximately 50 percent above the current level. Delivery promise fulfillment from vendors is ultimately expected to increase 99.9 percent. Incoming delivery lead time is projected to decrease from 64 to 30 days and scrap cost is projected to decrease from 1 to 0.2 percent. Many intangible benefits are also expected to occur from JIT purchasing implementation.

With such positive results in areas that are important to American manufacturing firms, many materials managers are looking at the potential benefits and are seriously considering adopting JIT purchasing practices. This book will help inform that decision.

PLAN OF THE BOOK

This book is composed of eleven chapters. Chapter 1 is an introduction describing the essential factors that have contributed to Japan's success in achieving high product quality and productivity. This chapter explains why changing the U.S. manufacturing production system is critical.

Chapter 2 defines the functions of materials management and traces the development of factors that influenced U.S. firms to make organizational changes in purchasing functions.

Chapter 3 presents an overview of JIT and traditional purchasing practices in the United States. Chapter 4 discusses the benefits, tangible and intangible, obtained by U.S. firms as a result of implementing JIT purchasing.

The next two chapters deal with the implementation factors and problems of JIT purchasing. Chapter 5 describes the common factors necessary for a successful implementation of JIT purchasing. Chapter 6 presents the major problems U.S. firms have encountered and recommends ways to overcome them.

Chapter 7 deals with JIT parts selection, delivery frequency, and transportation costs. Chapter 8 presents strategies for designing a transportation system to meet the JIT materials delivery requirements.

Treating the purchasing function as a "quality and productivity center" through the successful implementation of JIT purchasing is discussed in Chapter 9. Chapter 10 describes the role of quality control in JIT purchasing. Chapter 11 is devoted to the impact of quality control techniques and JIT on quality cost.

This book is based in part on information gathered by the authors from two separate studies. Both studies used a cross-sectional field survey of U.S. manufacturing firms that had implemented JIT purchasing and statistical quality control (SQC) techniques. In the first study, a survey questionnaire was sent to 52 firms; 21 responded. In the second study, a survey questionnaire was sent to 1000 firms; 205 returned completed questionnaires.

Information was also obtained from company documents, professional associations, and through personal interviews with purchasing managers, production managers, quality control managers, engineering and design managers, and transportation and traffic managers, in the following companies:

General Motors Corporation (Buick Division)

Hewlett-Packard Company (Greeley Division)

Nissan Motor Manufacturing Corporation U.S.A. (Smyrna Plant)

Kawasaki Motors Manufacturing Corporation U.S.A. (Lincoln Plant)

The Goodyear Tire & Rubber Company (Lincoln Plant)

Control Data Corporation (Omaha Plant)

Honda of America Mfg., Inc. (Marysville, Ohio)

Matsushita Industrial Company (Division of Matsushita Electric Corporation of America, Chicago, Illinois)

Boeing Aerospace Company (Kent, Washington)

Sony Manufacturing Company of America (San Diego Plant)

ACKNOWLEDGMENTS

The writing of this book was made possible by the contributions of a number of individuals and organizations. Dozens of managers in many companies provided useful information and shared their expertise with us, but it is not possible to acknowledge all of them by name. Certain individuals, however, made significant contributions and they deserve special appreciation.

First, we owe special thanks to Mr. Takehiko Saeki, President of Kawasaki U.S.A.; Steven M. Horonec, Arthur Andersen and Company; Jim Heckle, Production Section Manager at Hewlett-Packard (Greeley Division); K. F. O'Donnell, formerly Inventory Control Manager, Nissan, U.S.A.; Charles G. McDougall, formerly Administrator—Materials Management, General Motors (Buick Division); and Roger H. Slater, Director of Quality Assurance at LTV Steel Company.

Second, we would like to thank purchasing, production, quality control, engineering and design, transportation and traffic managers in the following companies: General Motors (Buick Division), Hewlett-Packard (Greeley Division), Nissan Motor Manufacturing Corporation U.S.A., Kawasaki Motors Manufacturing Corporation U.S.A., The Goodyear Tire & Rubber Company (Lincoln Plant), Control Data Corporation (Omaha Division), Honda Manufacturing U.S.A., Matsushita Company U.S.A., Sony Manufacturing Company U.S.A., and Boeing Aerospace Company.

Third, we thank those individuals who provided formal review and guidance: Jerry A. Viscione, Harriet B. Stephenson, Diane L. Lockwood, C. Patrick Fleenor, Rex S. Toh, and other colleagues in the Albers School of Business, Seattle University, Eileen I. McKillop (Boeing Company), Fred H. Tolan (President of Tolan Freight Traffic Services), and Judith M. Bentley (Consultant). Special thanks go to Patty Connell for her graphic design.

A. Ansari
B. Modarress

CHAPTER 1

Why Have Japan's Product Quality and Productivity Increased?

Japan's quality and productivity success can be attributed to its management style, the use of technology and innovation, and its manufacturing techniques.

FOR MANY YEARS Japan's success in achieving a high level of product quality and productivity growth has been unmatched by any other advanced industrial nation, especially in automobiles, cameras, large-scale integrated circuits, optical fibers, and television sets. The essential factors behind the success of the Japanese can be characterized by three basic factors: Japanese-style management, technology and innovation, and manufacturing techniques as shown in Table 1–1.

WHAT IS JAPANESE-STYLE MANAGEMENT?

Japan's success during a period of high inflation, high unemployment, slow economic growth, and decreased corporate profits in

TABLE 1–1. Effects of the Integrated Japanese System on Quality and Productivity

Management Characteristic	Japanese Management Practice	Effect on Quality and Productivity
Management style		
Consultative decision making	Decision making is employee participative; information flows from bottom up; focus is placed on defining the problem; many possible solutions are explored.	More responsibility is placed on employees, and on creating commitment and harmonious relationships among all participants.
Human resources	Long-term investment in human resources is emphasized, along with continuous on-the-job training supplemented by formal classroom study.	Various continuous training programs improve job-related skills and adaptability to new technology.
Long-term employment	Life-time employment system exists for employees up to age 55.	Strong commitment and loyalty are developed between employee and company.
Long-term planning	Top management pursues long-term achievement of organizational goals.	Middle and lower management personnel are encouraged to exercise creativity in developing intermediate objectives.
Technology and innovations		
Automation, robotics	New technological changes are introduced and adopted.	Automation and robotics are not considered threats by employees. Productivity increases and product quality is higher.
Manufacturing techniques		
Statistical quality control	SQC is used to make the product correctly the first time.	Amount of effort required to produce the product reduced, leading to a more efficient allocation of scarce resources.
Just-in-time	JIT systems are implemented to eliminate waste.	Product quality and productivity improve through elimination of waste.

the United States has stimulated much interest in Japanese management style, which has proven to be the foundation of Japanese product quality and productivity success.

What we know today as Japanese-style management is in part a refinement of ideas and findings about human motivation and satisfaction that were originally developed in the United States. The Japanese adaptation of these ideas represents a dramatic departure from traditional concepts of management to a new field of human endeavor. The approach has emerged from McGregor's theory of the human side of enterprise, Likert's process theory, Simon's decision theory, and others. This emphasis on human resources has, for the most part, been neglected by American management.

The Japanese management system can be referred to as an "ideology-driven" process of management. Management by ideology emphasizes superordinate organizational values and philosophies, long-term strategic goals, a two-way (i.e., top-down and bottom-up) communication system, cooperation and harmonious relationships, functional structures, strong commitment and loyalty to the organization on the part of its members, and a consultative decision-making process.

Consultative Decision Making

In the United States, top executives are perceived as professional managers who are capable of making key decisions and achieving organizational goals through personal judgment, initiative, and creativity. Generally, the decision-making process is "top down" through a hierarchical chain of command. The strength of this system is its quick decision-making capability. The system is prompt and impersonal in adjusting decision errors. However, it lacks an inspirational quality in management, and the importance of the human side of decision making is often neglected.[1]

In contrast, Japanese executives play key roles in shaping decisions and responding to ideas, but they are not considered key decision makers in the same sense as American executives. The tasks of Japanese top management are to make suggestions, improve initiatives, and encourage ideas resulting from the bottom-up process. Management is also responsible for creating an organizational environment in which subordinates are always encouraged to seek better ways to perform their work.

Decision making within the Japanese management style is a participative or consultative approach involving not only top management but also workers at the lowest level of the organization. Blue-collar workers' participation in quality control activities may include autonomous control over job site operations.[2] A Japanese company on average has about six times more people in problem-solving positions than an American firm.[3]

One of the key elements in decision making is that the Japanese managers are hungry for information, and they focus on defining and analyzing the problem, whereas the American manager places more emphasis on problem solution. The definition of the problem and various alternative solutions are usually discussed throughout the Japanese organization until a reasonable consensus is reached. Focus is on understanding the problem, with the desired end result being specific action and behavior from everyone involved.

Another key feature of Japan's consultative approach is that it allows a "bottom-up" decision-making process, a flow of information and initiative from the low level of the organization to the top level. H. Takeuchi pointed out that the "bottom-up" decision-making process constitutes the backbone of the Japanese productivity system. Often upper management sends a proposal to a lower-level organization where input proceeds in a bottom-up approach to the top levels of management.[4] The end result is that employees perceive they have the ability to make changes and do not feel far removed from top-level management. The Japanese manager believes that initiative for improvement within an organization should come from those closest to the problem. Thus, it makes good sense to elicit change from below.[5] Once a solution is selected, implementation is immediate, with wholehearted support from all key individuals.

Human Resources

A key characteristic of Japanese management is strong emphasis on human resources and the maintenance of harmonious relations. Perhaps among the most significant elements contributing to Japan's success in high product quality and productivity growth are continuous training and development of employees and the concern of top management to satisfy the social and secu-

rity needs of employees. The primary reasons for intensive training are:[6]

1. Improvement of job-related skills
2. Orientation of new employees to high performance standards
3. Instillment of company philosophy (top-down, through
   long-term training)
4. Promotion of dedication to continuing self-improvement

The Japanese organization offers various types of continuous
training programs on the job and in the classroom for employees
at all levels. The average training time for Japanese employees in
most large organizations is one day per week. For instance,
Nissan Corporation boasts a very successful seven-year training
program for incoming college graduates.

Although it appears that many American corporations have
spent millions of dollars on capital investment or in research and
development to solve quality and productivity problems, they
have neglected a long-term investment in human resources. The
quality and productivity problem in the United States will not be
solved by pouring money into equipment and R&D.[7] The secret
may lie in ongoing training.

Long-Term Employment

The long-term employment commitment on the part of Japanese
companies is one of the most striking characteristics of Japanese
management. It is of great importance in achieving a high rate of
productivity growth and product quality. Yet many American
companies object to the long-term employment concept because
they are concerned about keeping workers on the job who have
become ineffective.

American firms often practice what is referred to as the
"neutron bomb mentality."[8] At the first sign of a business difficulty, management "zaps" the human resources to save the build-
ings, machines, and equipment. Nothing wears the emotional and
motivational fabric of employees faster than this type of practice.
It is no wonder that many American employees job-hop frequently and have little long-term commitment to their organizations.

Most of the larger Japanese companies have a lifetime employment system for male employees up to age 55, and this stable employment system creates a "family" spirit. Japanese workers commit themselves to one company for their entire working careers and agree not to leave during bad times. The company agrees, in turn, to take care of its employees. This practice develops loyalty, harmony, and permanent relationships between employees and the company. Long-term employment builds trust, understanding, and a sharing of the overall values and objectives of the organization among employees. As a result, the organization's problems and goals become the employees' problems and goals, so they are personally challenged to solve those problems and achieve those goals.[9]

Hall pointed out two characteristics found among Japanese employees as a result of this long-term employment commitment. First, workers are more flexible as a result of job rotation; second, the workers do not fear automation. These characteristics have helped increase quality and productivity.[10] Japanese employees seem to adapt more readily and eagerly to advanced technology than do American employees, whose unions often raise objections to labor-saving techniques. In Japan, the opportunity to work on new equipment is seen as a way to prepare for future promotions. Also, the long-term job security provides a general work mentality conducive to making important management decisions for the long term.

Long-Term Planning Horizon

In the United States, management tends to be less willing to practice long-term planning and is more concerned with the existing market than Japanese management. American managers emphasize short-term planning in order to meet quarterly profit projections and to impact stock value. Hayes and Abernathy have noted that this focus on short-term planning is a major source of America's current quality and productivity problems.[11]

In contrast, the most consistent feature of Japanese top management is the pursuit of long-term growth. They are willing to put more emphasis on the longer time horizon to develop new products or markets and seem to be less preoccupied with shorter-term objectives. Based on this stable management philosophy, middle and lower management personnel are encouraged to exercise their creativity in developing intermediate objectives such as level of profit, market share, research and development, human resource development, and operational efficiency.

WHAT TECHNOLOGICAL INNOVATIONS HAVE BEEN MADE?

A number of observers attribute Japan's high product quality and high rate of productivity increase to their comparative ease in applying technological innovations, including robotics, computers, and flexible manufacturing systems. Although Japan has, in the past, been a major importer of such technologies, it is now emerging as a major exporter of these technologies, as well as an exporter of management and organization techniques. According to a study by the Tokyo office of the American Chamber of Commerce, U.S. technology is rapidly being overtaken by the Japanese in twelve important areas, including advanced ceramics, optical fiber, and large-scale integrated circuits.

Some argue that the Japanese are not inventive but rather are adaptive and clever borrowers, obtaining most of their good ideas from the West. For example, from 1950 to 1970, Japanese firms entered into 15,000 contracts to purchase Western technology.[12] The important point, however, is that they appear to introduce and use new technological developments in their productive systems more successfully than the West does. According to Vogel, the Japanese believe it makes sense to purchase foreign technology even if the costs initially seem high. In retrospect, the Western technology was obtained at bargain prices, allowing companies to concentrate their research on adapting the technology to increase their organizational efficiency and profits, which in turn resulted in their economic success.[13]

Although many technological innovations that Japan now exports were originally developed and used in the United States, Japan has become the primary user of these technologies. For instance, Japan is the pioneer in the use of robots, and roughly 70 percent of the world's 100,000 robots are in Japanese factories.[14] In recent years, many American firms such as General Motors and Ford have sent their executives to observe the use of robots at Nissan Motor Company in Japan.

Use of robots, computers, and flexible manufacturing systems in Japanese firms has increased productivity and improved product quality. For instance, at Toyota Motor Company, robots are operated using microcomputers, resulting in six times the efficiency of U.S. automakers. In another example, a typical die change on a major stamping in the Japanese auto industry takes about 5 to 10 minutes, whereas in the United States the same job takes about 6 to 12 hours. The Japanese company can thus change dies as frequently as required to meet the production schedule while minimizing inventory levels.

Our discussion here is not intended to suggest that Japanese technology is more advanced than that of the Western nations or that the Japanese use more sophisticated or superior technology in their factories. Hayes's study of six Japanese manufacturing factories indicated that "the general level of technology sophistication . . . observed was not superior to (and was usually lower than) that found in comparable U.S. plants."[15] However, his research suggests reasons for the Japanese success in introducing and applying new technology. These answers may lie in the areas of management style, human resource management, and employment.

American managers realize that the application of new technology and automation can greatly improve product quality and productivity, but such innovations have not always met with acceptance by U.S. workers or their union representatives. The introduction of a new technology may require changes in the nature of some jobs, adoption of new skills, and even job elimination. Technological advances are often perceived as a threat to the existing work situations.

In Japan, because of the long-term employment system and trust between management and workers, it is much easier to introduce new technology, as there is less resistance on the part of workers. A survey conducted during 1980–1981 among Japanese firms that had introduced robotics in their factories indicated that in most of the companies "personnel made surplus by robots were being transferred to creative divisions such as designing or development."[14] Thus, it is not surprising that shared acceptance of the value of technological change is greater in Japan than in the United States. This relatively easy adoption of a new technology has been a key contributor to Japan's productivity growth.[16]

WHAT MANUFACTURING TECHNIQUES DO THE JAPANESE USE?

Many American experts identify two key factors in Japan's high product quality and productivity growth rate: a more efficient allocation of resources (such as time, labor, materials, etc.) and a revolutionary quality control system. The force that shapes the organization of the quality system is statistical quality control (SQC). These factors—the efficient allocation of scarce resources and the SQC program—are completely consistent with one another, and together constitute just-in-time (JIT) philosophy.

The objective of JIT is to eliminate waste and to make the product correctly the first time. This in turn reduces the amount of effort required to produce the product, leads to a more efficient allocation of scarce resources, and provides a base for long-term productivity growth.

In the past few years, U.S. manufacturers have begun to realize the product quality and productivity benefits of SQC. Adopting SQC techniques for manufacturing process control has produced immediate benefits. For most, however, the potential value of SQC in the design phases (product design and production engineering) and manufacturing support areas (quality control at suppliers, distribution centers, information centers, and consumer services) has remained unrecognized.

The philosophy underlying JIT was developed in Japan. It was introduced in the early 1950s by T. Ohno, Executive Vice President of Toyota Motor Company, and perfected by Toyota in Japan. The idea was formalized into a management system when Toyota wanted to meet the precise demands of customers for various models and style configurations with a minimum of delay.

Schonberger, a U.S expert on Japanese management, has described the concept of the JIT manufacturing system in comprehensive terms:

> Produce and deliver finished goods just in time to be sold, subassemblies just in time to be assembled into finished goods, fabricated parts just in time to go into subassemblies, and purchased materials just in time to be transformed into fabricated parts.[17]

A primary objective of the JIT manufacturing system is the improvement of product quality and productivity through the elimination of waste. Waste is defined as anything other than the minimum amounts of equipment, materials, and workers that are absolutely essential to production. This suggests that in order to have a pure JIT system, production and purchasing activities must be synchronized. In other words, the production system is not complete without adopting JIT purchasing practices.

WHY CHANGE THE TRADITIONAL MANUFACTURING PRODUCTION SYSTEM?

Manufacturing is the foundation of the American economy. The manufacturing sector influences other economic segments, including service, government, and public utilities. Contrary to general belief, without a healthy manufacturing sector, we cannot sustain a healthy service economy. To restore American prosperity, a substantial fraction of capital and labor must be shifted to flexible systems of production. The prerequisite for flexible manufacturing systems is adoption of SQC techniques and the JIT system.

To make such a shift, Reich says, "American manufacturing management must unlearn 70 years of conventional wisdom about how to run a manufacturing business. Failure to do so could lead to a serious reduction and possible elimination of basic manufacturing in the United States."[18]

American managers generally believe that the goal of achieving a flexible manufacturing system conflicts with the goal of achieving high product quality and productivity. According to Wheelwright, American managers argue that "because both are valuable and because the achievement of one conflicts directly with achievement of the other, trade-offs are unavoidable."[19] Japanese managers, on the other hand, have realized from the beginning that flexibility in the production system and work force allows manufacturing to react very quickly to changes in market demand for products and models. Flexibility in production factors, such as equipment, design, material handling, work force, and the administrative time needed to change products and capacity, can lead to high quality and productivity.

One of the most important factors related to the United States decline in international market share is inferior product quality. Productivity correlates directly with quality; as one goes up so does the other. Prior to the 1970s, U.S. electronics, chemical, steel, and automotive industries dominated markets all over the world and maintained their industrial superiority through high quality and technology. In fact, as Dr. Juran pointed out, a product labeled "Made in USA" used to be a distinct asset to product salability.[20] In the early 1970s, however, a significant number of American firms began losing market share because of their declining product quality. This decline was closely related to using short-term cost cutting approaches instead of finding real solutions to production problems.

Increasing competition from Japan has forced American managers to seek ways to upgrade product quality. Several prescriptions have been offered. Dr. Juran described the massive quality training and improvement efforts undertaken in Japanese industry and advocated U.S. industry implementation of similar programs. These programs, with upper-management support and leadership, are key factors for improving quality. Dr. Deming suggested that American management has to absorb some of the principles of statistical quality control.[21]

We believe the ultimate solution to production problems is incorporation of the elements mentioned above and adoption of the JIT system. JIT's ultimate result is better quality with lower manufacturing costs.

SUMMARY

Not long ago, U.S. managers were proud to have Japanese business leaders visit their plants to see how work was efficiently accomplished. Now American executives are genuinely concerned about the Japanese business threat, especially in several important high technology areas. Just as the Japanese have learned from the United States, Americans can learn much from the Japanese.

What can American managers learn? The Japanese have achieved the world's highest level of worker productivity growth and quality through their management style, adoption of new technology and innovation, and manufacturing techniques.

The real strength of Japan is operational efficiency—efficiency based not on modern technology or factories but rather on simplicity, flexibility, and common sense. That is the JIT system. We believe the consideration of the JIT manufacturing system with its unique aspect—JIT purchasing—is a positive way to meet the Japanese challenge. Chapter 2 discusses the importance of the role of purchasing in the success of firms.

CHAPTER 2

Why Has Purchasing Become So Important?

Purchasing has assumed much greater importance in the organizational structure in the last twenty years.

IN THE EARLY 1960s, Lewis predicted dramatic changes in the future of the purchasing process. Ammer, in his classic article on materials management organization in 1969, suggested that the purchasing organization structure would blossom because of two significant forces: electronic data processing and a systems approach to management.[1] These expectations began to be fulfilled in the mid-1970s in U.S. manufacturing firms and came to fruition in the early 1980s, especially in the auto industry. During the past two decades, in fact, there have been more changes in the functions of purchasing than had occurred in its first 130 years.

Purchasing systems existed in earlier organizational structures, but at a fairly low level on the organizational chart. Purchasing's primary functions were regarded as strictly clerical, and were limited to sourcing, pricing, and delivery. During the mid-1970s, many firms increased the role of purchasing in the decision-making process by moving purchasing managers up to the executive level. Now, purchasing personnel are involved in many other functions, including new product planning, development of engineering specifications, and plant and capital equipment decisions.

This chapter's focus is the overall concept of materials management (which includes purchasing), its importance to the success of a firm, the evolution of traditional U.S. purchasing processes, and some of the major factors that influenced organizational changes in purchasing functions. The term "traditional" U.S. purchasing will be used, as distinct from "just-in-time" purchasing.

WHAT IS MATERIALS MANAGEMENT?

The concept of materials management, originally developed by Babbage, dates back as far as 1832. Babbage perceived the critical importance of having a key official responsible for selecting, purchasing, receiving, and delivering all the articles required for manufacturing.[2] In 1950, the General Electric Co. was the first company to develop and implement the function of materials manager, to be in charge of coordinating the complex movement of materials to, through, and out of the factories.

A decade later, manufacturing managers gave considerable attention to the materials management concept and it became an important function of the organization. One of the major reasons materials management became so important was cost:

> Historically, more analysis and control have been placed on the expenditure of monies for personnel, plant, and equipment than on materials. For manufacturing organizations, materials related costs have grown to be the largest single expenditure.[3]

The U.S. Department of Commerce's Census of Manufacturing for 1988 provided evidence for this: it reported that the majority of industries spend an average of 57.9 percent of their sales revenue for materials and services from outside sources. Thus, more dollars are spent for materials and services than for all other expenses combined, including wages, salaries, depreciation, and taxes.

The conclusion of a study done by Centamore and Baer in 1971 indicated that most companies have changed their organizational structure and have formally adopted the concept of materials management in order to:[4]

1. Lower operating costs
2. Centralize purchasing under a single responsibility
3. Reduce inventory
4. Increase purchasing power
5. Improve functional efficiency in all areas
6. Reduce purchase price

Miller and Gilmour have found that practitioners develop different materials management organizational structures based on individual corporate objectives. Four types of structure have been identified:[5]

1. Classically integrated
2. Distribution oriented
3. Supply oriented
4. Manufacturing oriented

The specific structure selected by a firm depends on a series of trade-offs. The individual top management style, markets, and critical elements of the manufacturing process will indicate which of the four materials management structures is correct for each organization.

The Functions of Materials Management

Materials management's responsibilities within organizations had already changed drastically by 1969. Yet there was no clear agreement on the specific functional organization of materials management. Many experts in the field of purchasing argued that materials management should control the acquisition, conversion, and distribution of materials flow from vendors to consumers, including raw materials, work in process, and finished goods. In 1969 Ammer opposed this broad view and proposed instead that the materials manager's functions should begin with the selection of suppliers and end when materials are delivered to their point of use. Ammer saw four advantages to this more limited view:[1]

1. Forced cooperation between purchasing and production control
2. Tighter inventory control
3. Efficiency in departmental coordination
4. Better communication between manufacturing management and various materials management activities

Just as academics disagree on the functions of materials management, practitioners, too, disagree as to precisely what activities materials management should include. Consequently materials management activities vary from company to company. Generally, the functions include all major activities that contribute to the cost of materials. The primary responsibilities of materials management are summarized in Table 2–1.

WHAT IS PURCHASING?

Purchasing is the single most important function of materials management. It is a specialized part of materials management, just as plant engineering is a specialized part of manufacturing. If the purchasing department has a problem, it becomes a company problem.

Responses to a 1975 purchasing survey indicated that more than one half of the companies questioned had either formal or informal materials management operations.[6] Regardless of the degree of formality, they reported purchasing functions as the most important aspect of materials management.

Purchasing has been defined by many scholars and practitioners. Here are two examples:

> The classic definition of purchasing's objectives is to buy materials and services of the right quality, in the right quantity, at the right price, from the right source, and at the right time.[7]

> The term "purchasing" simply describes the process of buying; however, in a broader sense, the term involves determining the need, selecting the supplier, arriving at proper price, terms, and conditions, issuing the contract or order, and following up to ensure proper delivery.[8]

TABLE 2–1. Scope of Materials Management Function

Activity	Primary Function	Secondary Function
Purchasing	Negotiate and assure availability of materials at the right time, right quantity and quality, right price, and right vendor	Select vendor, expedite, create favorable vendor relations with other company functions, such as receiving and engineering
Inventory control	Assure the maintenance of an adequate and balanced inventory of parts and materials with a minimum investment	Keep the records of parts and materials used in the production process and on order
Production control	Establish the total production schedules for parts and materials to facilitate production	Calculate the requirements for parts and materials using bill of materials and specifications supplied by engineering
Traffic	Select carriers, determine the total transportation costs, and reduce overall transportation costs	Check the incoming freight, outgoing freight, and internal plant transportation
Materials handling	Accept, handle, and physically move materials to production area	Reduce handling costs per unit of material from one location to another
Receiving and storage	Identify, verify quantity, inspect quality, prepare reports on incoming materials and physical storage of all materials	Provide services to other functions, protect materials against pilferage, and distribute all items.

Purchasing responsibilities vary among organizations, depending on their size and range, from the simplest tasks, such as preparation and payment of invoices, to very complex tasks, such as obtaining prices and negotiating purchasing contracts. It is important that the purchasing activity be centralized and responsibility be assigned to a specific department.

Purchasing should have full responsibility over several major functions defined by the National Association of Purchasing Management as ascertaining prices, negotiating purchasing

TABLE 2-2. Areas of Purchasing Responsibility

Main Function	Primary Emphasis	Methodology
Ascertaining price	Obtain the best price possible	Price indexes Competitive bidding Two-step bidding Negotiation
Selection of suppliers	Deal with dependable sources of supply	Capacity to produce Quality and quantity Financial stability Product testing
Negotiation of purchasing contracts	Negotiate effective contracts where both sides agree to bargain	Negotiate price, delivery, quality, and specification
Expediting of orders	Focus on the follow-up of orders	Review status of order Visit vendors' plant Write letters Telephone
Supplier relations	Develop a good relationship with suppliers	Mutual buyer-seller participation Buyer-seller mutual continuous relationship

contracts, selecting suppliers, expediting orders, and maintaining supplier relations. These functions are summarized in Table 2–2.

HOW HAS PURCHASING DEVELOPED IN THE UNITED STATES?

Many U.S. manufacturing firms have recognized that purchasing is as important to the success of an industry as finance, marketing, engineering, personnel, production control, and quality control. Until very recently, however, little was done to formalize the purchasing process.

The first article on purchasing appeared in the literature in 1915 when the magazine *Purchasing* (then called *The Purchasing Agent*) and the National Association of Purchasing Management (NAPM) (then the National Association of Purchasing Agents—NAPA) began their operations. The growth of the NAPM organization and the continued publication of *Purchasing* have been closely associated with the rise of purchasing as a profession.

In many firms during the 1960s, purchasing was considered a clerical function. Emphasis shifted in the early 1970s toward being more of a "profit center." Focus shifted again in the early 1980s, when the Japanese just-in-time purchasing concept was introduced in the United States. We now propose that just-in-time purchasing be considered as a "quality and productivity center." (See Chapter 9.) Table 2–3 summarizes these important events in the development of purchasing.

TABLE 2–3. An Historical Perspective on Materials Management and Purchasing Development

Time	Event
1832	Charles Babbage develops the first materials management concept.
1915	The magazine *The Purchasing Agent* (later, *Purchasing*) emerges. National Association of Purchasing Agents—NAPA (later the National Association of Purchasing Management—NAPM) is founded. Top management begins making major purchasing decisions. Plant foreman often makes minor purchases. Scientific purchasing begins.
1929	NAPM develops a set of standard procedures for buying and selling.
1939	Goodyear makes innovations in physical distribution management to control all finished products handling activities.
1951	Stuart Heinritz's *This Business of Buying* defines purchasing as a critical function.
1960s	Negotiation techniques, learning curves, cost/price analysis, inventory control, PERT/CPM networks, buyer training, and supplier evaluation become tools increasingly used by purchasing people. Purchasing function is considered a profit center. First MRP is developed at American Bosch Company; orders tend to be in large lot sizes.
1970s	Oil embargo, materials shortages, and escalating fuel and materials costs contribute to an increased focus on the importance of purchasing. Purchasing as a specialized task has been pushed to top level in organizational structures.
1980s	Japanese just-in-time purchasing concept is implemented by many U.S. companies; orders tend to be in small lot sizes.

WHAT FACTORS INFLUENCED ORGANIZATIONAL CHANGES IN PURCHASING FUNCTIONS?

The dramatic changes predicted by Lewis and Ammer occurred during a relatively short period. A study conducted in the 1960s showed that only 3 percent of manufacturing firms had altered their organizational structure to make purchasing a separate functional area.[9] During the mid-1970s, U.S. companies were operating in an environment characterized by product shortages, inflation, recession, high interest rates, excessive inventories, and a changing pattern of demand.

By then, hundreds of firms had altered their organizational structures by increasing purchasing's responsibility in the decision-making process. A study of 300 of the Fortune 500's largest industries indicated that during this period about 50 percent of the companies had expanded purchasing's scope of responsibility within the organization and had moved it to the executive level.[10] Chrysler's purchasing department, for example, reported directly to the president, not to manufacturing. Manufacturing had to advise purchasing when problems occurred. Also, purchasing was totally responsible for the quality of parts and for assuring that sufficient supply was delivered on time.

Why did these changes occur? Bonfield and Speh concluded from their research that many changes were related to sophisticated techniques such as computer use, planning needs, value analysis, and vendor analysis.[11] Miller and Gilmour in their 1979 article "Materials Managers: Who Needs Them?"[5] suggested that this rise in organizational position resulted from the significant changes in the business environment between 1967 and 1978. Some of these factors, in roughly chronological order, are as follows:

1973 Oil Embargo

Most companies were surprised by the sudden increase in the cost of materials during the 1973 oil crisis. The embargo created two problems: First was an enormous increase in the cost of operating petroleum-dependent engines. Second was tremendous shortages in basic industrial areas that were dependent on crude oil for sustaining their operations. Shortages in commodities like steel created a domino effect throughout all types of industries.

This situation forced manufacturing industries to reexamine their purchasing strategies within the organizational structure; it triggered the sharp increase in the importance of purchasing functions. It dramatically altered firms' long-term cost structures and made gains from not holding material very attractive. Control of inventory and material transport took on a new importance.

Double-Digit Inflation

The increased rate of inflation accompanied by high interest rates during the 1970s affected the entire manufacturing sector. The most significant effect was on purchasing, which was responsible for about 60 percent of product costs. According to Baily and Farmer, during this time manufacturing industries were forced to adopt "hand-to-mouth" stockholding policies, a term Japanese management describes as the just-in-time philosophy, and long-term planning for material requirements and purchasing costs became difficult.[12]

How did companies respond to these inflationary pressures? A 1978 national survey of U.S. buyers, CEOs, and purchasing managers showed that more than 75 percent of the companies increased their long-term purchasing contracts. More than 60 percent favored a tightened inventory control strategy as an ideal solution. Table 2–4 presents some of the important strategies used by the companies during this period of high inflation.[13]

TABLE 2–4. Purchasing Strategies During Period of High Inflation

Strategy	Percent of Respondents
1. Help improve production efficiency	85
2. Increase long-term purchasing	78
3. Tighten inventory control	60
4. Increase long-range planning	45
5. Consolidate purchasing	39
6. Expand value analysis	30
7. Increase hedge buying	22

Higher inventory carrying costs, related principally to the jump in interest rates, pushed the companies away from traditional inventory thinking toward purchasing smaller quantities and carrying a lower safety stock. A study conducted by Gaither in 1981 supported this change.[14] He examined the impact of inflation upon order quantities and order points and found that for most materials it was preferable to hold lot sizes constant and slightly reduce safety stock levels.

Shortages of Some Materials

It was no secret in the mid-1970s that the materials supply situation was rapidly becoming worse. The shortage of materials, both short and long term, made purchasing procedures and policies more important to the long-term survival of the company.

In 1975, a survey conducted by Lalonde and Lambert indicated that the most serious problems perceived by purchasing managers during a period of shortages were:[15]

1. Maintaining a balanced inventory
2. Containing the cost of raw materials for manufacturing
3. Obtaining accurate information on supply and delivery dates from vendors
4. Minimizing transportation costs
5. Avoiding inconsistent delivery of raw materials
6. Minimizing shortages of raw materials for manufacturing

Elevating purchasing to a top management function was considered the most effective strategy for coping with material shortages. A survey conducted before and during the shortage period (June 1973 to June 1974) among purchasing directors of Fortune 500 companies showed a dramatic change in the scope of purchasing responsibilities. For instance, purchasing responsibilities for negotiation increased 32 percent; for new sources of supply, 45 percent; in forecast materials needs, 52 percent; inventory control, 31 percent; new product development, 33 percent; and long-range planning, 42 percent.[10]

The regrouping of organizational structures and the movement of purchasing decisions to the top level was more evident in the U.S. auto industry than elsewhere. General Motors, for example, implemented the task-force approach as a part of its reorganized corporate purchasing department.

> Under the purchasing director, GM's forward planning group uses teams of five or six purchasing staffers to make studies. Team members come from both corporate and division staffs. According to the director of raw materials purchasing, the data developed within forward planning is transmitted to divisional purchasing, which in turn feeds it to engineering and manufacturing.[16]

American Motors Company has developed supply availability forecasting groups headed by the purchasing director. These groups help AMC prepare a strategy for shortages rather than relying entirely on tactics and improvisation. Chrysler has also grouped similar tasks under the purchasing director and called it their "commodity planning group."

Lead Time

An internal factor that pushed purchasing to the top of the organization was lead time. Lead time tends to be considered a noncontributory cost factor, but long lead times affect total material-related costs.[17] The lead time syndrome—long lead time stretchouts and consequent inventory buildups—is one of the most difficult problems for purchasing people to cope with. Wight described the problem in his 1981 book *MRP II:*[18]

> As vendor backlogs picked up, vendors quoted longer lead times. Customers, in turn, ordered more to cover themselves out over the longer lead time, thus increasing the backlogs—causing another increase in lead times.

He suggested the use of computer-based material requirements planning (MRP) to help solve these problems. Others have pointed out, however, that the implementation of MRP alone cannot solve the long lead time problem. A 1976 survey showed that, in general, only 75 to 80 percent of materials were delivered on time.[19]

The solution can be found instead in purchasing strategies. It became necessary for manufacturing firms to make adjustments in purchasing strategies, which resulted in changes in organizational structures.

Product Quality and Productivity

As all these factors have pushed purchasing into a greater role in decision making, so have the problems of declining product quality and productivity contributed substantially to changes in purchasing. From 1971 to 1982, the annual rate of increase in manufacturing output per employee in the United States dropped from 6.1 percent to 1.2 percent.[20] American managers have speculated widely about the causes of this decline: an increase in the price of crude oil, rising government regulations and intervention, union resistance to technological advances, congressional labor laws and policies, unfair marketing practices by foreign competitors, and lack of capital investment. A study conducted by McKinsey and Co. indicated, however, that only 15 percent of the variables affecting productivity are external to the firm; 85 percent are internal variables under the control of management.[21] It is within the individual firms, then, that solutions must be found.

The troubling productivity decline is symptomatic of more serious problems within companies such as the low quality of manufactured products and the high cost of manufacturing in the United States. These two problems represent a devastating force that has dampened U.S. productivity growth, but they are so embedded in traditional manufacturing processes that they have gone largely unrecognized.

Many experts and managers have attempted to assimilate different strategies to improve product quality and productivity in manufacturing firms. Among these strategies is an increase in purchasing's functions, one of the last remaining hopes.

This important strategy, however, was not realized prior to the introduction of the JIT purchasing practice in the early 1980s. It is not surprising to see significant efforts on the part of manufacturing firms now to improve their product quality and productivity through adopting the concept of JIT purchasing practices.

SUMMARY

Undoubtedly, the roles and responsibilities of purchasing have increased over the past several years, particularly in the decision-making area. This increase was the result of significant changes in the business environment between 1967 and 1978. Shortages of raw materials, long lead time, inflation, and a decline in product quality and productivity prompted these changes in the organizational structures of many manufacturing firms. They also resulted in an expansion of the basic activities of purchasing.

In a period of turbulent economic conditions, changes in purchasing practices are crucial to the current and future competitive advantage of firms. Adopting JIT purchasing practices appears to be the key in this case. JIT purchasing practice versus traditional purchasing practice will be analyzed in detail in Chapter 3.

CHAPTER 3

How Is Traditional Purchasing Different from Just-In-Time Purchasing?

Purchasing activities under traditional and JIT practices are the same, but they differ in approach.

WHAT IS THE JIT PHILOSOPHY?

JIT MANUFACTURING is one of the distinct features of a system that has contributed substantially to Japan's high product quality and productivity. The practice of JIT reflects its title. Materials are purchased or parts are produced in an exact quantity and just as they are needed.

JIT manufacturing works very efficiently under different economic conditions. Efficiency is achieved primarily through (1) complete support and cooperation of suppliers, (2) commitment of every person from the top to the bottom levels of the organization, and (3) a series of changes in the manufacturing process: purchasing small lot sizes, smoothing production, designing flexible processes, standardizing jobs, and employing an information system called kanban for ordering and delivery.[1]

The primary objective of the JIT technique is reduction of cost through the elimination of waste. Waste is defined as anything other than the minimum amounts of equipment, materials, workers, and time that are absolutely essential to production. Typically, from 15 to 40 percent of the quality cost for almost any American product is for imbedded waste. JIT demands that inventory be kept to a minimum. Extra supply increases inventory costs and ties up capital that could be invested elsewhere.[2] According to Ford Motor Company, every dollar's worth of parts carried in inventory costs the company 26 cents, mainly in interest and insurance. It costs U.S. automakers $8.5 billion to carry excess inventory to produce 11 million cars compared to $800 million in the Japanese auto industry to produce the same number of cars.[3]

JIT practice is not limited to inventory control and production systems but is also concerned with a very important aspect of manufacturing—purchasing practices. Under the JIT system, materials are purchased in very small quantities, with frequent deliveries, just in time for use. The actual parts needed for one day's operation in a manufacturing process or assembly line are supplied by in-plant sources or suppliers for immediate use. This chapter will contrast JIT purchasing with traditional purchasing by taking a closer look at the major activities of JIT purchasing in U.S. firms.

HOW DO PURCHASING PRACTICES DIFFER UNDER JIT?

Purchasing activities generally include all of the functions involved in the procurement of material, from the time need is determined to receipt and use of the material. Purchasing activities vary considerably among manufacturers, depending on the size of the firm. Generally, purchasing should have full or partial responsibility for several major activities, regardless of the organization's size:

1. Establishing lot size
2. Selecting suppliers
3. Evaluating suppliers
4. Inspecting incoming products

5. Negotiating with suppliers
6. Determining mode of transportation
7. Setting product specifications

All of these activities are approached differently in traditional purchasing and in JIT purchasing. Table 3–1 provides a summary comparison of both systems. Paperwork and packaging are other important related aspects of JIT purchasing.

Establishing Purchase Lot Size

Traditional purchasing practices rely heavily on a just-in-case concept. Large batches are purchased just in case there are serious disruptions in supplies. Most firms also purchase parts in large quantities rather than in small quantities because they consider shipping and handling costs a constant, regardless of the size of the load. Their justification for this practice is lower shipping and handling costs and discount rates.

JIT purchasing practices, on the other hand, emphasize the purchase of minimum lot sizes, preferably piece for piece. This allows tighter control over inventory, which eliminates the large stocks of parts between process stages. Under the JIT purchasing practice, obtaining small lot sizes is considered important enough to warrant overcoming the obstacles of higher freight costs and loss of discount rates. Several strategies, such as freight consolidation and dealing with local suppliers where possible, are effective in reducing total freight costs under JIT purchasing (see Chapter 7).

Selecting Suppliers

The most important decision a buyer makes is supplier selection.

Of all the responsibilities of the purchasing officer, there is none more important than the selection of a proper source. Regardless of how competent the purchasing officer may be to advise the engineering or production departments on matters of quality determination, how helpful he may be in describing the quality desired, how effectively he may supervise inventory control, how carefully planned is his office routine, or how accurately he may be able to forecast price trends, unless he can locate dependable and progressive sources of supply and can secure and maintain their active

TABLE 3–1. Comparative Analysis of JIT and Traditional Purchasing Practices

Purchasing Activity	JIT Purchasing	Traditional Purchasing
FULL RESPONSIBILITY		
Establishing lot size	Purchase is in small lots with frequent deliveries.	Purchases are made in large batches with less frequent deliveries.
Selecting suppliers	A single source of supply is selected for a given part, in close geographical proximity; with long-term contract.	Multiple sources of supply are selected for a given part, with short-term contracts.
Evaluating suppliers	Product quality, delivery performance, and price are emphasized; no percentage of rejects from supplier is acceptable.	Product quality, delivery performance, and price are emphasized; about 2% rejects from supplier are acceptable.
Negotiating with suppliers	Primary objective is to achieve product quality and a fair price through the long-term contract.	Primary objective is to achieve the lowest possible price.
PARTIAL RESPONSIBILITY		
Inspecting incoming parts	Counting and inspecting of incoming parts is reduced and eventually eliminated.	Buyer is responsible for receiving, counting, and inspecting all incoming parts.
Determining mode of transportation	There is concern for both inbound and outbound freight and on-time delivery. Delivery schedule is left up to buyer.	There is concern for outbound freight and lower outbound costs. Delivery schedule is left up to supplier.
Setting product specifications	Buyer relies more on performance specs than on product design. Supplier is encouraged to be innovative.	Buyer relies more on design specs than on product performance. Suppliers have little freedom in design specs.
RELATED ASPECTS		
Paperwork	Less time is spent on formal paperwork. Delivery time and quantity level can be changed by telephone call.	A great deal of formal paperwork is required. Changes in delivery date and quantity require purchase order.
Packaging	Small standard containers are used to hold exact quantity and to specify the precise specs.	Regular packaging is used for every part type and part number with no clear specs on product content.

interest and cooperation, the rest of his contributions will go for naught.[4]

A key feature of JIT purchasing practices is dealing with a small number of nearby suppliers—ideally single sources of supply—for a given part. Strong differences have always existed between those who advocate multiple sourcing and those who support single sourcing. The issue remains a major disagreement between JIT and traditional purchasing supporters.

Proponents of multiple sourcing argue that using more than one source of supply gives certain advantages:

— A greater degree of flexibility in technical areas
— Protection in times of shortages against failure at a supplier's plant
— Competition among suppliers in order to secure the best possible price and products

Furthermore, some suppliers are reluctant to become the sole supplier of one company.

Advocates of single sourcing offer the following advantages:

— A minimum investment of resources such as buyers' and engineers' time
— Consistent quality, because when buyers deal with fewer suppliers and involve them in the early stages of program design, suppliers can provide consistently high quality products
— Lower costs, because overall volume of items purchased from any one supplier is higher
— Special attention from suppliers, since buyers represent large accounts
— Minimal amount spent to provide tooling for suppliers
— Easily scheduled deliveries since all orders are placed with one supplier
— Long-term relationships, which encourage supplier loyalty and reduce the risk of an interrupted supply of parts to the buyer's plant

This last advantage is regarded as the most important reason for single sourcing. E. Hennessy, CEO at Allied Corp., explained[5]:

Purchasing must cultivate sound relationships with its suppliers so inventories may be reduced to minimum practical levels and quality of supply may be such that rejection of material is essentially eliminated.

For those who have implemented JIT purchasing, the advantages of single sourcing outweigh those of multiple sourcing. With respect to location of sources of supply, England stated, "Seventy-five per cent of buyers prefer to buy from local sources, and a substantial percentage of these indicate that they are willing to pay more or accept less satisfactory quality or service to do so."[4] Under JIT, geographical location of the supplier is important but not at the expense of quality.

Evaluating Suppliers

Evaluation of actual sources of supply is another important, continuing process in a good purchasing department. Purchasing management defines its objectives in terms of meeting manufacturing's material requirements with the best price, quality, and delivery; naturally management would like to know how it is doing in relation to its goals.[6]

A study conducted among 273 purchasing managers listed 23 factors to consider in evaluating a potential supplier. Product quality and delivery performance were ranked extremely important. Price structure was considered merely important.[7]

The method for evaluating suppliers varies with the nature, complexity, and dollar value of the competitive items purchased. Although numerous types and modifications of supplier evaluation programs currently are used in the United States, most possess three distinctive features with respect to the assessment and control of quality. One is simply to check the supplier's record for each shipment as to whether required product specifications have been met. This is usually measured as the percentage of rejections to total material shipped. Another method is to make monthly or quarterly tabulations of the percentage of the supplier's materials rejected by the buyer during that period. Another approach is a regularly scheduled review of quality performance conducted by the buyer, suppliers, and the engineering department.[8]

Evaluation of the suppliers' delivery performance is based on responses to inquiries, on-time delivery, special services rendered, and other factors. Measurement of special services rendered is quite subjective, as Aljian has pointed out, but it is nevertheless valuable.[6]

Under traditional purchasing practices a typical vendor delivery rating scheme might consist of categories such as top, good, fair, and unsatisfactory. The supplier's delivery performance would be tabulated and rated monthly.

JIT purchasing practices emphasize the importance of product quality, supplier relationship, delivery performance, and price, very much in this order. Although traditional purchasing practices focus on most of these factors as well, the order and degree of emphasis varies dramatically. Under traditional purchasing, for example, supplier evaluation has focused on the product being purchased, not on the buyer-supplier relationship.

Also, whereas with traditional purchasing many companies accept a 2-percent reject rate from suppliers, JIT purchasing permits no such percentage of rejects because the supplier is responsible for delivering just the right number of items. For instance, when Hewlett-Packard asked recently for a large sample of a component part, it subjected its potential suppliers to intense reliability testing. The best Japanese supplier had .003 percent unreliability; the best American supplier tested at 1.8 percent unreliability.[9]

Negotiating with Suppliers

Differences between traditional and JIT purchasing practices also exist in the negotiating and bidding process. Since typical buyer preference in traditional purchasing is to deal with multiple sources of supply, the bidding process implies that the lowest bid will usually get the contract. In fact, the whole objective in bidding from various sources is to obtain the lowest possible price. Most buyers provide very exact and rigid product specifications for prospective suppliers, so lowest cost usually becomes the only basis for the buying decision. The supplier typically offers very short-term contracts based upon competitive price.

With potential JIT suppliers, many purchasing departments have established different policies and guidelines for handling the bidding process. The objective becomes not just to negotiate for the lowest price but also to establish a very close relationship with the supplier. In fact, the lowest qualified bidders generally will not get the contract. Rather, the supplier most likely to be awarded a contract is the one who can provide consistently high product quality with no incoming inspection, deliver on time, work with the buyer to solve problems, and agree upon a "fair" price for both parties.

The bidding specifications are less rigid and suppliers are usually encouraged to be innovative in meeting buyers' specific needs. In JIT purchasing, an informal type of value analysis tends to receive special emphasis. In negotiating a JIT purchase agreement, the potential supplier receives the buyer's engineering drawings (with "loose" specifications) and responds with a bid price. The buyer then typically visits the supplier's plant to go over the bid in detail—that is, to conduct an informal value analysis (value analysis "on the fly"). The objective is to identify just where the highest costs are incurred by the supplier. Often the buyer can adjust the material specs in a way that will lower the supplier's cost, thus permitting him to reduce his price. This approach eliminates the need for suppliers to go through annual competitive rebidding. The purchasing manager at the Buick Division explained, for example, that about one-half of their 85 major suppliers have been working with the Buick Division for more than thirty years. Therefore, it is unnecessary to have these suppliers go through an annual rebidding process in an effort to save a few dollars.

Inspecting Incoming Parts

With traditional purchasing, the receiving department is responsible for receipt, identification, piece-by-piece counts, and inspection of all inbound freight for quality in accordance with product design specs. In fact, responsibility for inspecting incoming products is almost invariably placed on the buying company.

Under JIT purchasing, this type of inspection is avoided, except for new parts and new suppliers. Instead, quality control is performed at the source by the supplier. This practice is achieved primarily by extending the quality inspection function back to the supplier and making sure that quality is built in before the part leaves the supplier's plant. As a result, suppliers often drive their delivery trucks straight to the assembly line.

One way to assure the delivery of high product quality is supplier certification, a program that certifies that quality specifications have been met before parts leave the suppliers' plants. Another effective method is regular auditing of suppliers' plants.

Determining Mode of Transportation

The transportation cost of inbound raw materials and component parts is an important factor, after labor and material considerations, for most manufacturing firms. Depending on the type of industry, the cost of inbound freight may be 50 percent or more of material cost. Thus, whether the transportation cost is paid directly by the buyer or included in the price, it must be evaluated very carefully.

In a survey conducted by NAPM in 1971 about 1,940 out of 5,539 members responded that the purchasing department was responsible for transportation in their plants.[6] Due to the complexities involved in types and costs of transportation, however, responsibility should be placed in a separate department designated as the traffic department. The responsibilities of the traffic department would include incoming freight, outgoing freight, and internal plant transportation.

In the traditional approach, the handling of inbound freight is indeed different from JIT purchasing. Primary responsibility for scheduling and delivery is generally left up to the supplier and the transportation company, regardless of whether the purchase contract states FOB destination (ownership of the goods passes to the buyer upon delivery) or FOB shipping point (ownership of the goods passes to buyer at the time of delivery to the carrier). Manufacturing traffic managers concentrate on outbound freight.[10]

Why don't many traffic departments concentrate on inbound freight? Because in most manufacturing firms, the traffic department's performance is measured by its success in lowering outbound transportation costs, not on inbound freight performance such as on-time delivery.

Conversely, one of the most important requirements in the implementation of JIT purchasing is on-time delivery. To meet this requirement, the buyer must design a transportation system compatible with JIT materials delivery schedules. Because of the complexities involved in transportation (such as method and routing of shipment), the traffic manager in any buying company should have complete control and responsibility for inbound as well as outbound freight. Such control becomes even more important under JIT.

JIT purchasing cannot be successful if the responsibility for inbound freight schedules is left to the transportation company, whose primary concern is maximizing profits. In a JIT environment, the traffic manager should be more concerned with on-time delivery than with achieving a lower inbound freight cost. To meet JIT delivery requirements, delivery dates and times, types of carriers, routing decisions, and shipping processes must be designated by the buyer company (see Chapter 8).

Setting Product Specifications

According to traditional purchasing practice, engineers spend a great deal of time and effort specifying and developing tolerances for almost every conceivable design feature of the end product. Purchasing people simultaneously review purchase requirements to make sure that all product specifications (specs) are defined, and then let suppliers know exactly what the buyer wants. Types of specifications commonly used in the United States are blueprints (design) performance and material specs.

Of these, buyers rely more on design specs—which describe and identify the composition of materials to be used, their size, shape, and method of manufacture—and less on performance specs. Although design engineers are responsible for developing these specs, they rarely interact with suppliers, leaving all procurement problems to the purchasing department. This usually reduces the feedback that design engineers receive from suppliers in the area of design or quality.

Under JIT purchasing practices, the buyer seeks advice and assistance on technical matters from suppliers in order to design better parts, achieve lower prices, and improve product quality and productivity. In fact, the buyer relies more on supplier performance specs and less on narrowly defined design specs. This gives the supplier more discretion to make recommendations and suggest innovations in discussions with the buyer. There is a strong feeling among some managers that relying on performance specs places greater responsibility on the supplier for satisfactory products. Additionally, work delays are avoided in the supplier's plant because there is more freedom in dealing with product design.

Related Aspects

PAPERWORK

In traditional systems, forms are required for nearly all phases of purchasing, such as requisitions, packing lists, shipping documents, invoices, and so on. These supporting documents require massive amounts of time; purchasing people spend more than 50 percent of their time on paperwork.

Frequent changes in order quantity and delivery times have forced purchasing people into a reactive, "fire-fighting" mode. They deal with immediate crises rather than trying to prevent future ones. This gives them less opportunity to solve problems with suppliers or to work together to improve cost efficiency, product design specs, and productivity.

JIT purchasing requires much less formal paperwork. Because deliveries are made several times a day, long-term contracts are used, and a simple phone call can easily change the delivery time or quantity level. Paperwork is reduced by the use of kanban cards.

U.S. manufacturers have traditionally used a push-based MRP system for their purchased parts. In the past few years, however, many have designed and implemented pull-based JIT systems utilizing kanban for purchased parts. Kanban is simply a card system used to "pull" inventory through a production line by attaching cards to parts containers to control the flow of materials. A special standard container is designed for each part type and part number. Each container holds a precise quantity, preferably a very small one. Kanban cards are used to signal deliveries of the type and number of units needed. Newman Foundries, for example, uses its own trucks to deliver aluminum castings in standard containers with kanban cards attached to the Chevrolet transmission division once or twice a day, and it does so without paper documentation. Newman was one of the first suppliers to deliver to GM without paper documentation.[11]

PACKAGING

A factor often overlooked in traditional purchasing practices is packaging specification and handling. Better packaging and precise listing of produce content not only reduce manpower requirements but also affect the buyer, distributor, retailer, and marketing and transportation departments. Ammer suggested that purchasing people should be concerned not only with the flow of materials into the plant and finished products out of the plant but also with product specification packaging and handling, which can be quite complex and costly.[12] As Aljian noted:

> Packaging improvements may consist of such a small thing as specifying smaller containers to permit one-man handling or to prevent losses due to opened, partially emptied containers, which permit loss, deterioration, or contamination.[6]

Under JIT purchasing small, reusable, standard containers are used for every part type and part number. Since the containers hold a precise quantity (no overage or underage), the following advantages are realized:

Precise specification of parts on the containers

Easy, accurate count of parts

Reduction of packaging costs

Reduction of waste

Under a new program to eliminate defective parts, the Xerox Corp. has emphasized better packaging and handling. John Stalk, their materials operations manager, says the changes evolved from a close relationship with suppliers and a mutual effort to improve their packaging.

SUMMARY

JIT and traditional purchasing practices include the same activities, but they differ in approach. For instance, JIT purchasing suggests that parts be purchased in small lots with frequent deliveries as opposed to the traditional practice of large lot sizes and infrequent deliveries. Dealing with a single source of supply for a given part is preferred under JIT but not under traditional practice.

During the next few years, there will certainly be a heightened level of interest among many U.S. firms in the implementation of the JIT purchasing concept. The difference in approach under JIT can provide great benefits, both tangible and intangible, as will be seen in the next chapter.

CHAPTER 4

What Are the Benefits of JIT Purchasing?

JIT purchasing results in benefits greater than those from traditional purchasing practices.

IN AN INCREASINGLY COMPETITIVE BUSINESS environment, many firms are focusing on JIT as a method of improving their financial posture. In 1980, according to the National Academy of Engineering, there was compelling evidence that the Japanese had lowered costs and improved product quality in more manufacturing industries than their U.S. counterparts. These results are uniquely associated with the practice of JIT purchasing.

Adopting these practices, however, requires significant changes in the way firms operate. Is it really worth it to go through these changes in order to implement JIT purchasing? Based on the evidence of Japanese productivity growth and the results of a survey conducted among U.S. firms, the answer is yes.[1]

The major benefits of JIT purchasing derive from several practices. First, long-term relationships create a cooperative environment in which buyers and suppliers can share their business strategies and the production goals of high product quality and productivity, profitability, and growth. The primary objective of JIT is to make the product right the first time and to produce the necessary quantity at the necessary time. This in turn reduces the amount of effort and resources required to produce the product and eliminates inventories, which leads to efficient allocation of resources and reduction of costs.

Long-term relationships with suppliers and continuous communication also eliminate the need for annual rebidding and allow the buyer to share design and manufacturing information with suppliers and work very closely together to meet product specs and cut costs. This practice leads to reduced manufacturing costs that will be directly reflected in purchasing cost/price.

Small lot sizes with frequent deliveries are the next step in achieving JIT objectives. Suppliers must be able to produce parts in small quantities and make frequent deliveries without having to maintain warehouses nearby. This may require changes in suppliers' manufacturing systems that add significantly to the benefits obtained from JIT purchasing. Such changes may include focused factories, group technology, design for automation, and setup reduction, which will be discussed in the next chapter.

The advantages of these changes for suppliers are improved product quality and process capability, ease of communication, and reduction in lead time, space, material handling, and inventories. These changes not only reduce unit costs and increase profitability (which are reflected in buyers' costs), they also help to increase flexibility and responsiveness to buyers.

Another benefit obtained from improving quality is the elimination of incoming inspection, a benefit that is not reflected in the purchasing price but is considered a cost saving for buyers. The success of this depends on suppliers' quality control programs. Implementation of quality control techniques during design, manufacturing process, and distribution results in high-quality products and process and lower costs. These benefits are shared by both suppliers and buyers.

Whereas Japanese firms have benefited from the advantages of JIT purchasing for many years, some U.S. manufacturers have only recently begun to realize these benefits. The next section describes the degree to which these and other benefits have been experienced in the United States, as revealed by our survey.

WHAT ARE THE TANGIBLE BENEFITS
OF JIT PURCHASING?

The potential tangible benefits of JIT purchasing are categorized into seven groups in Tables 4–1 and 4–2. The most important benefits among the companies that we studied (21 companies responded to the questionnaire and 10 others were interviewed) were purchase material turnover, delivery promises met, and average delivery lead time.

Purchase Material Turnover

Sixty-two percent of firms reported an increase in inventory turnover. Prior to implementation of JIT purchasing, inventory was

TABLE 4–1. Current and Anticipated Tangible Benefits of JIT Purchasing

Benefits	Pre-JIT	Current	% Improvement	Future
Scrap cost as a percentage of total purchase dollars	9.7	5.9	40%	1.5
Purchase item inventory as a percentage of total purchase dollars	46.5	32.1	31%	21.6
Vendor response time to implement changes (days)	39.0	28.0	28%	19.0
Percentage of buyer time spent on expediting	33.0	23.0	30%	10.0
Purchase material turnover during a given period	6.7	13.2	97%	24.4
Percentage of delivery promises met	67.4	82.7	23%	97.6
Average delivery lead time (days)	77.0	64.0	17%	23.0

TABLE 4–2.   Tangible Benefits of JIT Purchasing Ranked in Terms of Importance

	Degree of Importance			
Benefits	Not Important 1 (%)	Less Important 2 (%)	Important 3 (%)	Most Important 4 (%)
Scrap cost as a percentage of total purchase dollars	—	24	38	38
Purchase item inventory as a percentage of total purchase dollars	—	10	60	30
Vendor response time to implement changes (days)	—	16	46	38
Percentage of buyer time spent on expediting	—	30	62	8
Purchase material turnover during a given period	—	—	46	54
Percentage of delivery promises met	—	—	14	86
Average delivery lead time (days)	—		57	43

replaced an average of 6.7 times during a given period. Under JIT purchasing, however, purchase material had a turnover of 13.2 during the same period, an increase of 97 percent. These companies expect inventory turnover to reach 24.4 in a given period in the future.

Delivery Promises Met

Sixty-seven percent of firms indicated that, prior to implementing JIT purchasing, suppliers met an average 67.4 percent of delivery promises. With JIT purchasing they met 82.7 percent, on average, of promised delivery dates, an increase of 23 percent. The buyers expect 97.6 percent of delivery promises to be met from their suppliers in the future.

Delivery Lead Time

Prior to instituting JIT purchasing practices, 67 percent of the firms had an average delivery lead time of 77 days. After implementing of JIT purchasing the delivery lead time was reduced to 64 days, a 17 percent reduction. It is expected that the delivery lead time will be reduced to 23 days, a 64 percent decrease, in the future. The reduction of average delivery lead time was considered the most important benefit of JIT purchasing.

Scrap Cost Reduction

Over 75 percent of firms using JIT purchasing indicated that, on average, scrap cost has been reduced from 9.7 to 5.9 percent of total purchase dollars, a 40 percent reduction, compared with pre-JIT practices. Upon full implementation, the scrap cost is expected to decline to 1.5 percent, an additional 74 percent reduction. Reduction in scrap cost was ranked as an important benefit of JIT purchasing.

Percentage of Purchase Item Inventory to Total Purchase Dollars

Forty-eight percent of firms indicated that the percentage of purchase item inventory to total purchase dollars had been reduced. The average reduction varied from 46.5 to 32.1 percent, a 31 percent decrease since the implementation of JIT. These companies expect a further reduction of 49 percent upon full implementation. Reduction in purchase item inventory also was considered an important benefit of JIT purchasing.

Vendor Response Time to Implement Changes

Sixty-two percent of firms showed a reduction in the time vendors take to implement requested changes. Prior to implementation of the JIT system, suppliers used an average of 39 days to implement changes (such as delivery time or quantity). Currently, however, it takes an average of 28 days, a reduction of 28 percent. These companies expect suppliers to be able to implement changes in 19 days, an additional 32 percent reduction. Vendor response time to implement changes is ranked as an important benefit of JIT purchasing.

Buyer Time Spent on Expediting

A less important tangible benefit reported by 62 percent of the firms was reduced buyer time spent on expediting. Prior to implementation of JIT practices, an average of 33 percent of buyer time was spent on expediting. With JIT purchasing, this time has been reduced from 33 to 23 percent, an average 33 percent reduction. In the future, buyers expect to spend less than 10 percent of their time on expediting, an additional 70 percent reduction. The same companies rated expediting as a less important tangible benefit of JIT purchasing.

WHAT ARE THE INTANGIBLE BENEFITS OF JIT PURCHASING?

Table 4–3 presents the results of the survey questionnaire with respect to intangible benefits of JIT purchasing. Table 4–4 shows their degree of importance to the companies. Despite varying degrees of improvements in the firms studied, more than 90 percent of firms agreed that areas showing greatest improvement were product quality, productivity, and success in encouraging vendors to meet quality requirements. Improved product design and reduction in purchasing paperwork were rated least important. The benefits ranked as most important were also those that had showed the most improvement.

SUMMARY

The studies of current practices in JIT purchasing among some U.S. manufacturers allow some tentative conclusions to be made concerning this new approach. In particular, the results provide information regarding the potential benefits of JIT purchasing and the extent to which these benefits are important to U.S. manufacturers.

Although it is difficult to quantify these benefits, firms that have adopted JIT purchasing systems have reported greater tangi-

TABLE 4–3. Intangible Benefits of JIT Purchasing

| | Estimated Degree of Improvement | | | |
Benefits	Little/None 1 (%)	Some 2 (%)	Much 3 (%)	Very Much 4 (%)
Improved product quality	—	26	31	43
Improved productivity	—	21	58	21
Success in encouraging vendor to meet quality requirements	5	11	53	31
Improved plant efficiency	5	21	48	26
Better production scheduling	––	37	37	26
More personal contact with vendor	6	31	37	26
Reduced need to inspect the incoming parts	16	21	37	26
Improved competitive position	5	37	48	10
Improved morale in production	11	31	48	10
Improved product design	21	58	16	5
Reduction in purchasing paperwork	26	48	21	5

ble and intangible benefits than those derived from traditional U.S. purchasing in inventory turnover, delivery promises met, a reduction in scrap cost, and a reduction in delivery lead time. Firms that have begun to use JIT purchasing expect even broader benefits when the system is fully implemented.

Companies considered improvements in intangible benefits—such as productivity, product quality, and success in encouraging suppliers to meet quality requirements—as most important. Improved product design and reduction in purchasing paperwork were rated least important. The benefits showing most improvement were also rated as the most important benefits of JIT purchasing, while the benefits showing least improvement were viewed as secondary.

TABLE 4–4.   Intangible Benefits of JIT Purchasing Ranked in Terms of Importance

Benefits	Degree of Importance			
	Little/None 1 (%)	Some 2 (%)	Much 3 (%)	Very Much 4 (%)
Improved product quality	—	—	11	89
Success in encouraging vendor to meet quality requirements	—	—	16	84
Improved productivity	—	4	23	73
Better production scheduling	—	10	45	45
Reduced need to inspect the incoming parts	—	5	56	39
Improved plant efficiency	—	6	41	53
Improved competitive position	—	10	34	56
Improved product design	4	17	34	45
Improved morale in production	—	7	58	35
More personal contact with vendor	—	23	47	30
Reduction in purchasing paperwork	5	28	67	—

Is JIT purchasing worth the trouble? Yes. With such positive results in areas that are important to American manufacturing firms of many types, U.S. companies should seriously consider adopting JIT purchasing practices. Chapter 5 describes the implementation process.

CHAPTER 5

How Is JIT
Purchasing Implemented?

Quality is the heart of JIT purchasing implementation; other aspects are just a matter of logistics.

WHEN THE CONCEPT OF JAPANESE JIT PURCHASING WAS INTRODUCED TO THE UNITED STATES IN THE EARLY 1980s, many companies were skeptical as to whether this new manufacturing philosophy could be successfully implemented here. Top management had a tendency to believe that although JIT purchasing made good sense for Japanese companies, it might not be appropriate here because of sharp contrasts in management style, manufacturing philosophy, social and cultural features, and, in some cases, size.

It did not take very long, however, for American companies to realize that successful implementation of JIT purchasing was possible. Many U.S firms have already developed and implemented their own version of JIT under different names, such as ZIPS (Zero Inventory Production System), MAN (Material-as-Needed), and Nick-of-Time. By any name, JIT treats purchasing the same way.[1]

Implementation of the JIT purchasing concept is a three-phase project. Phase 1 is a learning process, which involves experimenting with JIT purchasing and trying to achieve incremental improvements by reducing inventories, eliminating waste, exposing problems, and responding immediately to them. According to the Automotive Industry Action Group, a proponent of the JIT effort in America, most U.S. companies using JIT in 1984 were in this phase.

Phase 2 consists of pilot programs. Typically, the pilot program begins with: (1) a few local suppliers; (2) a few part numbers, representing a high dollar investment and low volume; (3) a few carrier companies; and (4) frequent deliveries (once or twice a week) directly to the assembly line. Starting the pilot program with a few local suppliers and a few parts increases the likelihood of success because problems such as poor supplier quality can be measured and late or early deliveries can be monitored and adjusted.

Success of the pilot program depends upon a group effort among managers in several departments who share the same goals. If members of the group have conflicting goals, their disagreement will influence the action of certain departments. In choosing the class of parts that are appropriate for the JIT program, for example, the finance department may favor the parts that have the highest impact on corporate profitability. The purchasing department may prefer other parts for different reasons. To make this program work the group must share the same objectives and work closely to influence their departments to pursue those goals.

The final phase is implementation. JIT purchasing must be designed to meet the needs of the individual company. However, some common factors that are critical to successful implementation were identified by the companies we studied. This chapter focuses on these factors, which fall into two basic categories: human and operational, as outlined in Table 5–1.[2]

WHAT ARE THE HUMAN FACTORS INVOLVED?

Human resources play a major role in the success of JIT purchasing programs. Studies indicated that top management's commitment and leadership, employee readiness, and labor union support are the most important criteria for success.

TABLE 5–1.   Factors Affecting the Implementation of JIT Purchasing

Factors	Recommendations
ORGANIZATION OF HUMAN RESOURCES	
1. Top management commitment and leadership	Obtain continuous top management commitment to and leadership of the program, in terms of both ideas and actions.
2. Human resources readiness	Prepare employees in every department and at all levels for the goals and objectives of the program. Also, prepare employees to learn different jobs.
3. Union leaders' support	Secure union leaders' support so that employees can be trained in different jobs and be flexible in job assignment.
ORGANIZATION OF OPERATIONAL FACTORS	
1. Purchasing philosophy	Adopt a new purchasing philosophy with the following components:
Lot sizes and delivery schedule	Purchase in small lot sizes with frequent deliveries. Select suppliers who can deliver high-quality parts in small batches.
Number of suppliers	Establish a manageable supplier network; reduce the number of suppliers to a few or a single source.
Long-term relationships	Develop long-term relationships with suppliers. Give suppliers long-term, flexible contracts.
Supplier involvement and support	Start supplier involvement prior to the implementation stage, so the supplier will be motivated to contribute to the success of the program.
2. Controlled transportation system	Establish buyer control over and responsibility for inbound freight schedules.
3. Efficient materials handling and receiving procedures	Eliminate formal receiving and incoming inspection.
4. Firm schedules for suppliers	Provide firm and accurate scheduling for suppliers.
5. Standard containers	Require suppliers to use standard containers for delivering parts.

Top Management Commitment and Leadership

The most important prerequisite for a JIT purchasing program is top management commitment and leadership. Upper-level managers are often not familiar enough with the JIT program to utilize their leadership in implementing it. After they have thoroughly familiarized themselves with JIT, they must publicize the corporate philosophy regarding JIT purchasing and their commitment to this program in the following ways:

1. Give program implementation the highest priority as an organizational goal.
2. Change the corporate culture and employees' attitudes toward the JIT program.
3. Provide sufficient resources and proper training for employees.
4. Establish a top-level steering committee, consisting of directors of manufacturing, personnel, engineering, purchasing, distribution, traffic, and quality control. This committee provides counsel, oversight, and direction to the company efforts.

As implementation gets under way top management must ensure that the intended company objective remains on schedule. At Nissan U.S.A., for example, the president put on the company uniform and spent time with workers on the assembly line to demonstrate his commitment to the success of the program. This is crucial in the initial stage of implementation when production may be halted due to a lack of parts or poor quality of parts delivered. At Kawasaki's plant in Lincoln, Nebraska and at the Hewlett-Packard Greeley Division, it is not uncommon to see assembly lines stop for a few minutes or even hours because of lack of parts. Kawasaki's philosophy has been that even if the lines must be shut down for a few hours, it is worth it in the long run.

Human Resources Readiness

Another important factor in the implementation of JIT purchasing is the support and commitment of every employee in every department, all the way down to machine operators.

Once top management realizes the potential benefits of JIT

purchasing for the company, all employees can be properly trained. In many companies top management believes that JIT purchasing will be more successful if the employees become involved at an early stage. When this does not happen, the result may be employees' unwillingness to contribute to the success of the program.

Early involvement includes preparing employees to: (1) understand the goals and objectives of the program, (2) accept changes within their work procedures and unlearn years of conventional wisdom, (3) accept cross-section training, learn different skills, and move from one job to another as the system requires, (4) accept more responsibility within their jobs, and (5) be active participants in the program by suggesting new ideas.

Union Leaders' Support

Cooperation between union management and company management in implementing JIT purchasing is also a vital prerequisite. When unions are involved, union officials' commitment to the program is important. JIT necessitates labor flexibility so that employees can be reassigned from one job to another as the system demands.

Often, such changes are perceived as threats to existing work situations and thus are strongly opposed either by workers or their union representatives. In companies where job descriptions are specifically defined, it is unlikely that JIT implementation will succeed without union leaders' support.

Fortunately, wage employees and union officials are now becoming interested in policies regarding employee involvement, commitment, long-term employment, and quality of work life, which all relate ultimately to the success of a JIT program. Not unnaturally, they are also cautious because they are uncertain about the effects of these changes on their jobs.

WHAT OPERATIONAL FACTORS ARE IMPORTANT IN IMPLEMENTING JIT?

Several operational factors were found necessary for successful implementation of JIT purchasing, including (1) a new purchasing philosophy which includes lot size, number of suppliers, long-term relationships, and early supplier involvement and support;

(2) a controlled transportation system to meet JIT delivery requirements; (3) efficient materials handling equipment and receiving procedures; (4) accurate and firm supplier scheduling; and (5) the use of standard containers.

New Purchasing Philosophy

When a company adopts the JIT purchasing philosophy, the role of the buyer changes. Basic functions (locating good suppliers, negotiating contracts, expediting orders, and following up to assure compliance with purchasing system standards) remain the same, but the response of the buyer changes. The buyer becomes more active, working very closely with suppliers to establish long-term relationships for better product quality and on-time delivery.

The new philosophy requires a consistently high quality of purchased parts. According to the Senior Buyer at Buick Division: "Quality is the heart of JIT purchasing implementation; other aspects, such as moving parts from point A to point B on time, are just a matter of logistics." Four factors have been identified as important in improving quality and thus implementing JIT.

PURCHASE OF SMALL LOT SIZES IN FREQUENT DELIVERIES

The hallmark of JIT purchasing is the steady purchase of parts in small lot sizes, rather than in large batches as is traditional under U.S. purchasing practices. Despite the strong indication in the literature that the geographical location of suppliers is an important criterion for effective implementation of JIT purchasing, the results of the survey did not completely support this contention. Only 9 percent of companies surveyed indicated that suppliers' geographical location is an *important* factor. Surprisingly, 53 percent responded that this is of *little importance* or *not important* at all. The transportation manager at Nissan, for example, explained his company will buy wherever possible, as long as suppliers provide high-quality products, on-time delivery, technical assistance, and fair pricing.

DRASTIC REDUCTION IN THE NUMBER OF SUPPLIERS

All the U.S. companies that have implemented JIT purchasing have drastically reduced their number of suppliers, to three or less for a given part. Without this reduction, JIT purchasing becomes unmanageable and strong long-term relationships with suppliers cannot exist. Having many suppliers for a given part forces purchasing personnel to concentrate on coordinating them rather than on the primary objective of improving quality.

In order for suppliers to be competitive and meet high quality standards, they must implement statistical quality control (SQC) techniques. A massive, continuous training and education program in the JIT purchasing philosophy must be initiated for suppliers, but fewer suppliers means fewer companies requiring training by the buyer's company.

There are several other important advantages in having a single or a few sources of supply:

1. *Higher quality.* A single source of supply can be managed more easily, giving the buyer more time to work closely with a supplier. This results in greater contributions from the supplier in areas of design and product quality.
2. *Better communications.* A single source of supply poses fewer communication problems. For example, only one source needs to be notified about changes in order quantity and delivery time for specific parts.
3. *Operational advantages.* A certain amount of production and paperwork time necessitated by changing from one supplier to another can be eliminated when dealing with a single source of supply.
4. *Cost reduction.* A single supplier can constantly contribute to cost-cutting ideas. The engineering people can spend more time working very closely with the supplier to reduce high costs.

LONG-TERM RELATIONSHIPS

Long-term and mutually beneficial relationships between buyer and supplier also contribute to improvement of product quality. Such relationships encourage the supplier to be more innovative and to economize in the production process.

More importantly, long-term relationships and flexible contracts encourage supplier loyalty and reduce the risk of an interrupted supply of parts to the buyer's plant. Also, there is a constant improvement in the system of production and services. Buick Division, for instance, has given its JIT suppliers 18- to 36-

mouth flexible contracts with the potential for renegotiation every 6 to 12 months in exchange for quality improvement and cost reduction.

EARLY SUPPLIER INVOLVEMENT AND SUPPORT

Another prerequisite for successful implementation of JIT purchasing is early supplier involvement and support. Ninety-five percent of the companies surveyed indicated that without early involvement and close cooperation between the buyer and suppliers, JIT purchasing will fail. The Buick Division senior buyer said: "The real owners of the plant are the suppliers." Buyers concentrate on educating and training suppliers for JIT purchasing.

Controlled Transportation Systems

An important requirement for JIT purchasing is on-time delivery. The buyer designs a transportation system compatible with JIT materials delivery schedules. Then, because of the complexities involved, such as methods and routines of shipments, the traffic manager in the buying company should have complete control and responsibility for inbound as well as outbound freight.

JIT purchasing cannot be successful if the responsibility for inbound freight schedules is left solely to the transportation company, whose primary concern is maximizing profits. In the JIT environment, the traffic manager is more concerned with on-time delivery than with achieving a lower inbound freight cost.

To meet JIT delivery requirements, the buyer company designates delivery dates and times, types of carriers, routing decisions, and shipping processes. In Chapter 8 we discuss the design of a transportation system to meet JIT materials delivery requirements. The majority of U.S. companies implementing JIT purchasing have transportation or traffic departments that control inbound freight delivery schedules.

Efficient Materials Handling Equipment and Receiving Procedures

Under the JIT system, huge receiving areas are no longer required for housing incoming materials. The manager, however, must ensure that the receiving and materials handling facilities are capable of supporting JIT delivery requirements. G. Isaac, of Touche Ross & Co., comments: "This might involve establishing a warehouse beside a key customer as a final assembly or staging point. Such a facility would lend itself to receipt of truckload quantities, coupled with frequent LTL or milk-run deliveries."[3]

When the formal receiving and inspection of incoming purchased materials is eliminated, suppliers can get as close to the assembly line as possible and deliver parts directly to the work station. Quality inspection at the supplier's plant greatly reduces the need for receiving inspections at the buyer's plant. Our investigation has indicated, however, that many companies still have not completely eliminated formal incoming inspection.

The Automotive Industry Action Group has suggested elimination of incoming inspection through certification of supplier quality. Under their "Just-In-Time in America" program, the buying company educates and trains suppliers with regard to quality assurance and quality control techniques. Subsequently, the supplier certifies that quality specifications have been met.

In addition to reducing incoming inspection costs, elimination of formal receiving operations results in less handling, a smoother movement of materials between stations, less time spent on the physical movement of materials from the time received until used, and less chance to damage parts.

A Buick Division manager stated that his division was in the process of eliminating the incoming inspection of all parts, which had required bringing in boxed parts, setting them down, moving them to storage, stacking them up, and then moving them back to where needed.

The Hewlett-Packard Greeley Division has adopted a new procedure to reduce handling for some bulky foam parts. According to its traffic manager, scheduling is arranged so that a trailer of foam inserts is at the receiving dock at all times. When one trailer is almost empty, the truck company is called. It delivers a full trailer within an hour and pulls away the empty one. Currently, the Buick Division has developed similar procedures to improve its efficiency in receiving and materials handling.

Firm Scheduling for Suppliers

Since one of the primary objectives of JIT purchasing is to have little or no inventory, suppliers must receive firm and accurate schedules so that materials can be secured and delivered in the right quantities at the right time.

Fifty-two percent of the companies we studied indicated that successful JIT purchasing depends on accurate production schedules with little fluctuation in quantities and delivery times. One technique used to back up the assembly schedule is the kanban system, which replaces purchase orders, vendor invoices, and receiving reports; the companies researched, however, have not yet integrated the kanban system in their operations.

Among the companies studied, suppliers who deliver parts on a JIT basis usually receive a firm monthly schedule of requirements, two to four weeks in advance, plus a one- or two-month tentative requirements schedule. A few trusted suppliers even have direct access to the buyer's computerized MRP system, so they can update their schedule constantly.

The buyer's schedule must be stabilized in order for the supplier to meet it smoothly. The Buick Division production manager explained that when schedules fluctuate as much as 15 to 20 percent, suppliers tend to believe the company does not know what it is doing; therefore they build extra inventory just in case a sudden schedule change demands more inventory than they have. Soon the suppliers start operating on their own schedules, no matter what the buyer company says the schedule is.

Utilization of Standard Containers

The use of standard containers for delivering parts or materials has many potential benefits. These benefits can be categorized into five groups: (1) easy identification of precise quantities and specification of the part number, (2) facilitation of receiving and materials handling procedures, which reduces manpower needs and prevents mistakes, (3) elimination of potential damage to the parts in and out of the plant, (4) reduction of packaging costs, and (5) reduction of waste, which results in clean work areas and saved space.

Among the companies surveyed, the number that require suppliers to use standard containers is very small, but a few were in the process of shifting to standard containers. The Buick Division, for example, is designing trailers that optimize space and meet JIT requirements for the Detroit area, where there is a heavy concentration of suppliers. Each trailer will have four tiers. When a trailer leaves the plant in the morning, the tiers are full of empty containers, arranged by suppliers according to the delivery sequence. When the trailer goes to the first supplier, empty containers are replaced by full containers. By the time the trailer returns to the plant, the tiers are full of containers of materials.

WHAT OTHER CHANGES WILL OCCUR?

Without a doubt, implementation of JIT purchasing practices causes fundamental changes in many systems, including:

1. Manufacturing layout
2. Production
3. Design and production engineering
4. Quality control

MANUFACTURING LAYOUT

Changes typically begin with plant layout. According to *Just-In-Time for America*,[4] manufacturing layout consists of:

Focused factory	—A manufacturing layout dedicated to the production of a single family of parts
Group technology	—An equipment layout dedicated to the complete production of a family of similar parts, one at a time, by linking all possible operations in the process
Design for automation	—A systematic way of simplifying operations for product design and production engineering
Set-up reduction	—A process of minimizing machine downtime during part number changeovers to facilitate small lot size

The advantages of focused factory, group technology, and automation are consistent improvement in productivity through improved quality, manufacturing flexibility, and increased operation capacity. Other advantages are reductions in lead time, space, operations complexity, materials handling, and inventory. The application of these techniques requires reducing the layers of organization, which ultimately leads to ease of communication and utilization of resources.

PRODUCTION

In order for production management to keep assembly lines operational and meet production schedules with zero or minimal inventory, the production and purchasing departments communicate frequently. The production department constantly shares information with the purchasing department so the buyer can ensure a smooth flow of materials from suppliers to assembly lines. Close communication also helps production systems in uniform scheduling, which is a planning method for resource allocation based on smooth, homogenized production flow.

This brings important changes in production policies and practices. Training in diagnosis and problem-solving techniques, including SQC techniques in day-to-day operations, helps production personnel anticipate problems and find ways to solve them rather than just follow the production schedule and live with the problems. To produce consistently high quality products and prevent defective parts, assembly line workers must be given authority to stop the production line when they cannot solve a problem within the operation cycle.

This concept was observed at the Kawasaki Lincoln plant, which is using kanban for the actual consumption and control of materials. In some of these plants, workers can stop the line if they cannot fix the problem by themselves. The assembly line is monitored by an overhead andon indicator board, with green, yellow, and red trouble lights and numbers to indicate the section with problems. Also, workers are trained to record the frequency with which system elements are replaced so that they perform preventive maintenance on their own equipment. If preventive maintenance fails, the employees can fix minor problems.

Production workers are also responsible for keeping the minimum amount of what is needed for production on the floor; keeping each tool, part, and material in a designated location; and keeping their own area and tools clean. Such responsibility creates an environment that minimizes equipment downtime during part number changeovers and facilitates small lot production.

DESIGN AND PRODUCTION ENGINEERING

Design and production engineering is another area that is simplified and highly integrated with production operations, purchasing, and marketing to achieve the strategic objectives of JIT purchasing. Design and production engineering cannot function as a separate area and must be an integral part of the system.

Design and production engineers work very closely with production personnel to understand production operations so that products and processes can be designed together for the production of a high-quality, reliable product. On the other hand, designers interact continuously with the buyer to find out fundamental expectations for the product and its application and to resolve problems with respect to specifications and standards. This arrangement results in closer coordination between the engineering and purchasing departments and leads to higher quality design.

QUALITY CONTROL

Another functional area that must change or modify its procedures to support JIT purchasing is the quality control department. Under JIT, the quality control staff is diverted from final inspection of manufacturing to prevention of defects. This total process control concept has been in effect at Hewlett-Packard, Nissan, Kawasaki, Buick Division, and the Lincoln, Nebraska plant of Control Data Corporation (CDC). By adopting JIT purchasing, the number of quality control inspectors at Kawasaki, for example, was reduced from 33 to 14.

This change clearly demonstrates that quality control staff members are not solely responsible for product quality; rather, this responsibility is shared by every employee involved in the manufacturing process. The quality control manager at CDC explained that over 90 percent of their employees have received formal quality control training and are directly involved in quality improvement programs.

Generally, quality control staff members work very closely with production workers and teach them various methods and techniques of SQC to identify and resolve minor quality problems. They also train suppliers in SQC so that they can use the production process to improve product quality. Production employees' knowledge and understanding of SQC reduces the need for quality control staff.

SUMMARY

Once companies have experimented with JIT purchasing and run pilot programs, successful implementation depends on several factors as summarized in Table 5–1. From the beginning, top management must understand, first, that JIT is not just a series of techniques. Rather it is a manufacturing philosophy which requires the support, commitment, and participation of human resources at all levels of the organization. It also requires fine-tuned planning among different departments within the organization as well as careful coordination with outside companies, such as suppliers and transportation companies.

Second, implementation of a JIT program is not an on-time effort with a distinct beginning and end. It is a continuous process. Third, JIT purchasing philosophy involves fundamental changes in corporate culture and employee attitudes, training program, and internal organizational structure. Some of the problems that can come with implementation will be the subject of the next chapter.

CHAPTER 6

What Problems Are Encountered in Implementing JIT Purchasing?

The most serious problems are not operational in nature. They are "people problems."

JIT HAS PRODUCED SUBSTANTIAL BENEFITS for firms that previously used traditional U.S. purchasing practices, as discussed in Chapter 4. Inventory turnover increased by an average of 97 percent; delivery promises met increased from 67 percent to 83 percent; and scrap cost declined 40 percent. Most important, our survey revealed that the greatest degree of improvement was in product quality and productivity.

While JIT purchasing has provided impressive benefits, major problems can also arise. Their significance will depend on a number of variables: type of materials purchased, type of product manufactured, type of manufacturing processes and facilities utilized, product demand patterns, and the corporation's culture and organizational structure. The most serious problems, however, are not operational in nature. They are "people problems"—

stemming from attitudes and orientation, past experience and practices, and the passive factors of interpersonal relations.[1]

In this chapter we focus on problems that seem to cause the greatest difficulty in implementing JIT purchasing. The seven significant problems we found in the firms we studied are presented in Table 6–1. These problems are explored in detail and recommendations to overcome them are proposed. Our recommendations are by no means exhaustive, but they encompass the most important points revealed by the firms studied. Each organization

TABLE 6–1.   Major Problems Encountered in the Implementation of Just-in-Time Purchasing

Major Problems	Recommendations
Lack of support from suppliers	Education and training of suppliers in JIT purchasing. Development of a long-term mutual relationship with suppliers
Lack of top management support	Motivation of top management through learning and actual analysis of results
Low product quality	Establishment of a quality management program aimed at early identification of critical quality characteristics during design, manufacturing, and engineering stages of the supply process
Lack of employee readiness and support	Emphasis on continuous long-term training of employees in JIT purchasing. Education of employees about company's main objective and the philosophy behind implementation
Lack of support from carrier companies	Drastic reduction in the number of carrier companies. Requirement of transportation services on a contract basis
Lack of engineering support	Constant coordination and cooperation among engineering, purchasing, and production departments
Lack of communication	Early involvement and high level of integration among purchasing, production, engineering, and transportation

will make appropriate modifications for its own style of manufacturing and its own unique culture and environment.

LACK OF SUPPLIER SUPPORT

The most significant problem involved in the implementation of JIT purchasing appears to be lack of cooperation from suppliers, especially as it concerns quality. Forty-seven percent of the companies studied indicated they had encountered serious problems with a number of their suppliers. Thirty-four percent of the companies indicated significant but less severe problems, and only 19 percent reported little or no problem with suppliers.

Discussions with managers revealed a number of reasons why suppliers do not fully support JIT purchasing programs:

1. *Little or no incentive for suppliers to adopt JIT delivery.* Suppliers do not generally want to commit to JIT delivery until they are assured greater benefits than are normally received in the traditional buyer-supplier relationship. Suppliers want to know why they should make a contribution to the success of this program when the primary benefits are realized by the buyer.
2. *Lack of commitment from buyers.* Suppliers have generally been treated as independent parties. Buyers often stimulate competition among several suppliers so they do not have to rely solely on a single source.
3. *Considerable strain on suppliers.* Suppliers are not accustomed to continuous scrutiny from buyers. Under JIT purchasing, they are constantly under pressure from the buyer to deliver good quality products in the right quantity on a continuous basis. The quality control manager at the Buick Division noted that pressure is always on suppliers. If they fail to deliver materials correctly the first time, they will get a second chance. If they still fail to meet the requirements mutually agreed on, GM searches for a new supplier.

Recommendations

Two strategies minimize these problems: (1) education and training of suppliers, and (2) development of long-term relationships with suppliers.

EDUCATION AND TRAINING

Perhaps the most important objective of education and training is to ensure that suppliers thoroughly understand the main purpose for implementing JIT purchasing in the buyer's organization. The senior buyer at the Buick Division explained that the primary purpose of Buick's JIT program is to attain a consistently high level of quality for incoming materials. Cost savings from reduced inventories are a side benefit. To achieve the main goal of JIT, a buyer must assume responsibility for educating and training suppliers.

Three major approaches are available to educate and train suppliers in JIT purchasing. The first consists of an intensive presentation and group class discussion of the JIT purchasing concept at suppliers' plants, including representatives from appropriate functional areas, such as production, engineering, traffic, and quality control. The second approach is continuous in-house training at suppliers' plants. The buyer's firm typically sends selected quality control and engineering personnel to their suppliers' plants and provides the required training and technical assistance (if necessary) to bring product quality up to the buyer's standards. The third approach is to schedule periodic "vendor days" conducted at the buyer's plant for all JIT suppliers to enhance their understanding of the cooperative nature of their relationship with buyers.

LONG-TERM RELATIONSHIPS

Buyers are encouraged to develop strong, long-term relationships with their suppliers through the use of flexible long-term contracts. The purchasing manager at the Hewlett-Packard Greeley Division reported that suppliers have certain expectations of buyers under the JIT concept. Some of the important expectations are summarized below:

1. A long-term business arrangement
2. A fair return on supplier investment
3. Adequate time for thorough planning
4. Accurate demand forecasts
5. Correct and firm specifications
6. Parts designed to match the suppliers' process capability
7. Smoothly timed order releases
8. A fair profit margin
9. Fair dealings with regard to price

10. A minimum number of change orders
11. Prompt payment of invoices

Once these expectations are met, buyers normally achieve reasonable cooperation and subsequent integration of suppliers into their JIT purchasing programs.

LACK OF TOP MANAGEMENT SUPPORT

Another problem that can hinder the success of JIT purchasing implementation is the failure of top management to support the program. Although 52 percent of the companies responding indicated little or no problem in gaining the full support of top management, 48 percent indicated that they did not have strong support of upper-echelon personnel.

There are several possible reasons for this lack of support. Top management generally tends to be less concerned with long-term planning arrangements and more concerned with existing markets and short-term profitability. Constant pressure from stockholders to maintain a high level of stable dividends often generates this shorter term view.

A second reason is skepticism. Some management people believe that JIT is not well suited to most American firms. Additionally, many general managers become frustrated with the magnitude of problems encountered and the sporadic results experienced during the initial phase of implementation.

Successful development of a JIT purchasing program requires top management's perseverance, patience, long-term commitment, and leadership.

Recommendations

How can top management be motivated to implement JIT purchasing programs? Two effective approaches have been observed.

The first focuses on education as a means to effect attitudinal change. Common activities include visits to other companies that have implemented a JIT program, attendance at seminars or workshops on the subject, and carefully selected reading in appropriate journals and trade magazines. In addition, various associations such as the American Production and Inventory Society (APICS), the Automotive Industry Action Group (AIAG), and the National Association of Purchasing Management (NAPM) have assumed positive roles in increasing top management's awareness and knowledge in this area.

The second, and perhaps most direct approach, is the use of positive JIT results experienced by other firms to convince general managers that the concept can also enhance their own company's competitive position. Many managers must see firsthand that JIT can be used successfully in the American environment before they are willing to provide the necessary support and leadership. They must be convinced of the following:

1. JIT purchasing is appropriate and can be implemented in the company.
2. JIT purchasing can improve the overall operation of their plants.
3. The potential benefits of JIT purchasing are broader than those of traditional U.S. purchasing.
4. JIT purchasing can improve product quality and productivity.
5. JIT purchasing can improve employee satisfaction.

Managers who visit Japanese or American plants that have implemented JIT can see for themselves. Once these benefits are demonstrated, top management will make the needed changes in the organization's human resources and operational functions, and implementation of the JIT concept throughout the organization will proceed more smoothly.

LOW PRODUCT QUALITY

A frequently encountered obstacle to successful implementation of JIT is the difficulty of obtaining high-quality materials from suppliers on a consistent basis. Fifty-three percent of the companies studied indicated this was their major problem. Twenty-eight percent reported some problems with regard to quality of parts purchased, and only 19 percent indicated no significant difficulty in obtaining materials of acceptable quality.

Inconsistent quality of purchased parts also constitutes a significant problem area for the companies we studied. When suppliers fail to provide material of adequate quality on a regular basis, down-line supply problems occur that may create a production stoppage or slowdown. This, in turn, may jeopardize the JIT purchasing program.

The causes of this problem appear to be (1) inadequate experience in supplier management, and (2) past manufacturing philosophies that allowed the acceptance of an excessive percentage of defects in incoming materials shipments.

Recommendations

The best way to resolve this problem is to establish a quality management program for suppliers aimed at early identification of critical quality characteristics during the design, manufacturing, and engineering stages of the supply process. Two ways to assure the delivery of high-quality products are: (1) development and utilization of a supplier certification program, and (2) utilization of a supplier plant audit.

When the buyer has established long-term relationships with suppliers and has found that their product quality is consistently reliable, it makes sense to place the primary responsibility for inspection and quality control with the supplier. An effective supplier quality certification program assures that the quality specifications have been met before parts leave the supplier's plant. In other words, the supplier takes "ownership" of quality requirements for the parts it delivers.

A second method in helping suppliers deliver high product quality is regular auditing of suppliers' plants. The supplier quality assurance manager at Nissan explained that six engineers regularly audit their local suppliers' plants and work very closely with them on quality issues. The main objective of this program is to improve quality through improvement of design and process engineering and subsequently to detect and minimize quality problems through statistical quality control.

LACK OF EMPLOYEE READINESS AND SUPPORT

A frequently encountered problem is lack of employee readiness and support. Many employees simply do not understand the concept of JIT purchasing. Thirty-eight percent of the companies surveyed reported some problems in gaining employee participation and support during the implementation stage. An additional 28 percent experienced major difficulty in this regard. The remaining 34 percent indicated no significant difficulty with respect to employee support in introducing purchasing programs.

There are some key reasons why implementation of JIT purchasing does not receive sufficient cooperation from employees.

1. *Resistance to a change in habits.* Employees who have performed a specific job repetitively for some years naturally find it difficult to change their perceptions and habits to coincide with those required in a different conceptual environment.

2. *Fear of job loss.* Employees always interpret the introduction of a new system as a threat to their jobs, since it often requires some changes in the nature of the job, adjustments in the workplace, adoption of new skills, and, in some cases, actual job elimination.

3. *Increased pressure and potential frustration.* To achieve successful implementation of any new system, management must place significant pressure on employees to do their jobs right the first time. JIT is no exception. In addition, the JIT concept requires individual employees to assume more responsibility for solving problems, and that, too, causes frustration. As the quality control manager at the Buick Division put it, "implementation of JIT is a mentality problem for employees."

Recommendations

Two different solutions help overcome lack of employee readiness and support. The first approach emphasizes long-term, continuous JIT purchasing training for all employees involved with purchasing and materials activities, even at the expense of short-term efficiency and profit. These training programs should teach specific new technical skills as well as the basic concept of JIT. On the job training is supplemented with classroom study. At Hewlett-Packard every employee receives formal training. Employees' knowledge is kept up to date with a program requiring every employee to spend several hours a week studying video tapes related to his or her area of work.

The second approach uses a broader orientation, focusing on

The second approach uses a broader orientation, focusing on the company's reasons for adopting JIT as well as the philosophy behind it. Ample time spent educating employees about the importance of JIT to the company's future success increases positive responses to the required changes. Everyone then understands his or her role in helping achieve the company's goal. Implementation problems can be reduced drastically if employees understand that successful JIT purchasing will be a major influence on the company's long-term growth and profitability and that each employee's personal future depends on the company's successful operation of its JIT systems.

LACK OF SUPPORT
FROM CARRIER COMPANIES

Many companies experience difficulty in obtaining cooperation from carriers with respect to inbound freight schedules. In fact, 53 percent of the companies surveyed had such problems; the remaining 47 percent reported no significant problem with carrier companies.

Historically, buyers in many firms have not given much attention to the purchase of transportation. Carrier services typically have been arranged by both buyers' and suppliers' companies on a less than systematic, ad hoc basis. The result has been that few buyers have developed long-term relationships with carriers that are able to provide unique services or highly structured delivery schedules for the buying firm. In most cases the carrier has "called the tune," and buyers have accepted what carriers were willing to offer. It is not surprising to find that delivery requirements of JIT systems are largely foreign to many carriers' modes of operation.

In the past, carrier companies did not take the buyers' schedules very seriously. They assumed that buyers had ample inventory and thus would not need the materials immediately. The traffic manager at the Buick Division related that the division usually placed several calls to a carrier company insisting that materials be delivered by the next day. When the carrier complied, the truck might sit in the receiving dock for several days before it was unloaded. As a result, the carrier company felt the buyer did not really know when he wanted the parts delivered.

Recommendations

Several steps can minimize problems with carriers and facilitate prompt JIT deliveries. The first step is to reduce the number of carriers used. This enables a buyer to purchase transportation services much as he or she buys materials. The buyer is able to place more business with each carrier selected and to work more closely with each in arranging mutually feasible delivery schedules.

In the case of purchases involving truckload or fairly sizable shipments, transportation may be purchased from a contract carrier. This type of arrangement lends itself readily to the development of specific contractual features to meet the unique service or delivery requirements of the buyer. In the past, for example, "Buick City" carriers did not keep their promises and shipments would fall behind schedule. Now there are penalty clauses in the contract for late shipments.

The third step for some buyers is an extensive computer interface with major carriers. Development of such a network makes it possible for participating carriers to update the buyer's information system as materials move through the carrier's system. The buyer's company can, in turn, easily monitor delivery activity and develop internal scheduling modifications if required.

The fourth step is to have all freight picked up and delivered on a scheduled basis. The buyer can then work very closely with each carrier's vendor to set up a pick-up schedule that will satisfy service requirements and minimize carrier costs. These steps are so general they can be adopted by any company.

Chapter 8 is devoted to the transportation network under JIT purchasing. The above recommendations and additional factors are discussed in detail.

LACK OF ENGINEERING SUPPORT

Lack of support and cooperation from design engineering personnel is another serious problem experienced by 39 percent of the companies. About 38 percent of the respondents indicated lesser problems in gaining engineering support.

Design engineering is primarily responsible for preparing

technical specifications for the materials a company buys. Unfortunately, this task often involves minimal interaction between design engineering and purchasing personnel. Purchasing people frequently do not have enough information about design features and constraints to discuss design or quality options with suppliers. The resulting technical interface with suppliers is often less than adequate.

Recommendations

The most desirable solution to this dilemma is the development of an operating climate that encourages and promotes a continuously high level of integration in all operations, including production, design and process engineering, materials control, and purchasing matters. The result of frequent interaction between engineering and purchasing is that, in many cases, suppliers with quality problems can solve them effectively and quickly with the appropriate buyer. This practice substantially increases the chance of JIT purchasing success.

LACK OF COMMUNICATION

Lack of communication within a firm's total operating system with respect to implementation of JIT purchasing represents another problem area. Effective development and implementation of JIT purchasing requires cooperation and integration of efforts from a number of important areas, such as materials management, manufacturing management, quality management, transportation, and production control. Ironically, significant problems were broadly reported in this area.

The major obstacle between purchasing and other areas such as engineering, design, production, and quality control is the difference in viewpoints. Engineers tend to be very cautious in specifying and developing tolerance requirements for every end item. Buyers, on the other hand, attempt to lower the engineer's performance limits and work with minimum standards.

Recommendation

Unfortunately, there is no easy solution to this problem. Resolving the lack of communication and coordination in JIT environments requires not only the continuous communication of purchasing personnel with all other personnel, but also that both engineers and buyers become more conscious of the overall objective of JIT. Design and process engineering must be an integral part of the production system, for example, and work very closely with purchasing, rather than functioning as a separate area. They must also work closely with production staff on the production floor to develop a product of high quality and reliability and make production flow smoothly. This is a responsibility purchasing management must assume, and it must call regularly on top management for leadership and support.

WHAT OTHER PROBLEMS CAN BE EXPECTED?

There are a few other factors that can cause serious problems and require careful attention when implementing JIT purchasing.

Government Contracts

JIT purchasing tends to direct itself toward the development of single sourcing. This, however, can cause a serious problem for manufacturing firms when the U.S. government is a major customer. Government agencies require a bidding process for government contracts; manufacturing firms must request quotes from a minimum of three suppliers for non "sole source" parts.

In the past few years, the defense industry has been the focus of congressional hearings which have resulted in a stricter interpretation of regulations and specifications. Under the 1986 Competition in Contracting Act both defense contractors and Department of Defense (DOD) agencies are required to implement major changes in their operations and procedures. This act requires competitive bids or justification of sole sourcing. The DOD is quite aggressive in advocating the use of competitive bids and it challenges the use of sole source supplies.[2]

Some companies have as much as 80 percent of their total sales directly attributable to U.S. government agencies or generated from sales to prime government contractors. Therefore, it is extremely important for the purchasing department to adhere to government rules and regulations. This obviously contradicts the JIT purchasing philosophy of establishing long-term relationships with a supplier and can be very difficult when a competing supplier tries to "buy" the business. If all things seem equal among the competitors, the contract must be awarded to the lowest bidder.

Since the U.S. government is unlikely to change its policies, the only solution is to give up JIT practices or government contracts!

Cost Accounting

Yet another problem involves cost accounting, a concept that was developed fifty or sixty years ago, when the principles of mass production created an operations environment of standard and stable products and technology. Management began to be concerned about maximizing productivity and efficiency of direct labor. Because labor was a large component in product cost, it was reasonable to consider overhead as a fixed expense and to allocate it based on labor. Since inventory was considered a valuable asset, management invested in it just as they did in facilities and equipment.

Because JIT changes a company's methods of production and purchasing, it also changes the values of production. Quality becomes a primary concern, as the simplification of production processes and product design brings a company closer to the goal of zero defects. Manufacturing productivity through JIT drives down production changeover costs to zero and economic order quantities to one. As flexibility increases, the need for an economic justification based on cost-per-piece diminishes. Fixed costs no longer can be spread over a high volume of identical products. Under JIT, inventory is a liability and the efficiency of operations is measured by the speed with which inventory moves through the plant. The relative role of labor will continue to decrease and product life cycles will become ever shorter.

What type of cost management system works in the JIT manufacturing environment? The answer is one that enables management to manage costs in a factory where there are no physical inventory counts, no work-in-process inventory, no hard-copy reports on receiving and shipping, and no purchase orders. In addition, the system should offer an incentive for the effective use of labor without traditional labor efficiency reporting or the mea-surement of individual work rates. Third, it should provide a means to achieve and measure the goal of continuous improvement in the manufacturing process. It should be able to measure and control costs at the level where they are incurred, and make and evaluate investment decisions over the entire life cycle of the product while including such components as flexibility, quality, and customer responsiveness. Timely reports, both financial and non-financial, from the factory floor must be relayed to the appropriate individuals. Last, cost management should be based on strategic and operational measures, rather than on traditional financial ones.[3]

Scheduling

In companies with only a few product lines purchased under JIT, purchasing is not controlled by the individual manufacturing lines. They do, however, control the scheduling function which determines the quantities and need dates of parts delivered from purchasing. Schedulers traditionally were required to interpret material requirements planning (MRP) screens and requisition parts according to the dates needed to produce the assembly. They were completely dependent upon lead times set by the purchasing department.

In a JIT environment, schedulers determine annual requirements for materials based on sales forecasts for the year. These requirements become input for weekly MRPs. Then schedulers develop their own method of determining supplier delivery requirements, which are MRP adjusted based on customer orders. If they allow too much material to be delivered there will be no place to store it. If they don't bring in enough material, the line will shut down, causing a loss of revenue.

Reducing lead times also depends on the relative accuracy of the marketing forecast. From the marketing point of view, however, the accuracy of the individual product forecast is not as critical as total sales. As long as business is good, marketing is not held accountable for forecasting errors. Thus information available for MRP may be inaccurate, which in turn destroys the flexibility of JIT. Buyer and supplier flexibility is required to respond to schedule changes.

Product Redesign

In many situations, a customer may require a product with specific configurations, thus turning a standard product into a "special." These configurations may include such things as changing the color of a case or incorporating changes that are specific to each order. Since it is sometimes impossible to predict these changes in advance of normal production cycles, the daily rate must be altered on short notice in order to make shipments.

In a JIT environment, however, a linear schedule is required to assure smooth production flows. When specially configured products are entered into the master production schedule with little or no notice, more specialized material must be held on the line in order to accommodate these special orders or finished products must be reworked. Both of these alternatives are costly but necessary in order to satisfy the customer. This buffer stock or rework would not be required if the master production schedule were not so volatile and if forecasts were more predictable.

Lead Time

Suppliers' long lead times are an exceptionally difficult limitation to overcome. Supplier lead time is 90 percent of queue time. In many buyers' companies today, raw material purchases are scheduled using MRP. Unfortunately, very few suppliers so far have agreed to reduce their lead times in order to support JIT efforts. As suppliers' lead times increase, the buyer's MRP becomes more "nervous" with respect to its accuracy. This, in turn, causes purchased part schedules to become quite volatile and leads to increased frequency of change order activity. All this weighs heavily on schedule instability. Buyers and suppliers must work together to reduce queue times and, thus, improve response times.

Suppliers' unwillingness to shorten lead times is not always unjustified. In many instances, the technology of the industry does not allow the benefits of JIT to be realized. In the printing industry, for example, lead times for the raw material of specialized paper have adversely affected lead times for the finished product, instrument manuals, which are currently running at twelve weeks.

Setup times in this industry can also be extremely lengthy.

The capital equipment available in this area and in many other industries is not yet amenable to quick setup and changeover. This is not expected to change soon because most firms cannot afford to invest in equipment that would allow for quicker setups.

SUMMARY

In addition to the benefits of JIT purchasing, U.S. firms have encountered major problems in the implementation process, including lack of supplier support, low product quality, and the like. Many of these problems can be resolved using appropriate strategies, and the lure of higher product quality and productivity justifies a continuing effort to overcome the obstacles. The next chapter will discuss strategies that reduce freight cost under JIT purchasing.

CHAPTER 7

How Are Freight Costs Reduced Under JIT Purchasing?

Choosing JIT parts and delivery frequency wisely will minimize freight costs.

THE HALLMARK OF JIT IS SMALL LOT SIZES. Parts that are purchased steadily in small lot sizes contribute to higher productivity in an organization through lower levels of inventory and scrap, high product quality, lower inspection costs for incoming parts, and earlier detection of defects.

Another important element of the JIT concept is daily delivery, whenever it is practical. A frequent and steady delivery scheme "forces" a number of desirable performance improvements to occur. Once daily deliveries begin, suppliers must target for the production of "perfect" parts, material must flow freely, paperwork must be perfect, and a host of other administrative factors must be handled correctly all of the time. This integrated process achieves three important goals:

1. Inventory is reduced substantially.

2. Space is managed effectively.
3. Problems that arise are resolved quickly.

As mentioned above, one of the most important aspects of JIT purchasing is the prospect of inventory reduction. Many American managers expect, however, that they will lose in additional freight costs what they save from inventory reduction. The main purpose of this chapter is to correct that misconception. The advantages of JIT purchasing include improvements in product quality and productivity, elimination of large warehousing costs and multiple exposures to handling damage and loss, and reductions in financing costs on inventories. These advantages are real and can outweigh increased inventory carrying cost.

Obviously a major disadvantage is that buyers may pay more freight cost, because shipments are based on assembly line needs rather than on weight. But buyers can reduce total freight costs if they select the parts to be purchased in frequent deliveries wisely. A strategy is outlined for selecting these parts and their delivery frequency. The traffic department can also reduce high costs with the strategies suggested in the transportation costs section at the end of the chapter.

WHAT IS A GOOD STRATEGY TO REDUCE COSTS?

In developing a program to reduce shipping and related costs, two important questions arise:

1. What classes of parts should be purchased in small quantities utilizing frequent deliveries?
2. What is the appropriate frequency of delivery for each of these parts?

The following sections detail an approach, or framework, for dealing with each of these questions. The approaches discussed here have been tested and have worked successfully for the companies we studied.

Selecting JIT Parts

To date, no American company has adopted the JIT purchasing concept for every production part used in its operation. In each of the plants surveyed, a relatively small percentage of parts are purchased on a JIT basis. Generally speaking, there are no firm and fast rules in making the determination. Although their basic approaches are similar, each of the firms determines its own decision rules, based on its unique set of operating and managerial factors.

Since late 1982, when Hewlett-Packard formalized its JIT purchasing program, the firm has utilized JIT for only about 45 items out of 4,000 production part numbers. Colorado Manufacturing Technology, one of Hewlett-Packard's suppliers located several hours from the Greeley plant, supplies flat ribbon cables on a daily basis. All other JIT parts are delivered on a once- or twice-a-week basis. The eventual goal is to attain daily delivery schedules for all these items.

At the Kawasaki plant in Lincoln, a sizable percentage of production parts are handled in a JIT mode. Approximately 80 percent of the JIT parts are received in lot sizes of 200 from the parent company, Kawasaki Heavy Industries, located in Japan. The balance of its JIT parts are supplied by U.S. firms, on either a daily or twice weekly delivery basis. Overall, Kawasaki's inventory of JIT parts runs at the two- to four-day level.

The Nissan plant located in Smyrna, Tennessee, has only one true JIT supplier, the Hoover Seats Company. Hoover delivers truck seats daily to the Nissan plant, which maintains no safety stock of seats at any time. Other quasi-JIT production parts used in the Nissan assembly operation are delivered twice a week from local suppliers. A sizable percentage of Nissan's parts, however, are supplied in large lots through the use of traditional purchasing contracts.

General Motors' Buick Division utilizes about 600 suppliers. Approximately 85 of these suppliers work under a JIT arrangement with Buick and deliver parts on a daily basis.

The firms surveyed have implemented their JIT purchasing programs on a partial and selective basis for two obvious reasons. First, dealing with and controlling a large number of suppliers in the JIT mode is an extremely complex and difficult task. A JIT purchasing program clearly requires a great deal of coordination and control activity between the buying and supplying organizations—and these activities require significant amounts of time to develop and manage.

The second reason is that the JIT approach does not necessarily produce significant benefits for all parts. Low-value parts, or volatile-usage parts (parts whose performance may vary under different conditions) can usually be handled quite effectively in a conventional purchasing mode.

How, then, do firms determine which parts to purchase on a JIT basis? The determination begins with a typical A-B-C Pareto-type analysis as described in the following paragraphs.

CLASS A PARTS

This class consists of high dollar investment material, typically high-tech parts and custom-made parts, and any part that represents a significant portion of inventory consumption over a given period of time. At Hewlett-Packard, for example, class A parts represent about 88 percent of dollars spent but only 3 percent of part numbers. This distribution suggests daily delivery for this class of parts and helps identify potential JIT suppliers.

CLASS B PARTS

This class includes all space-intensive parts, such as packaging materials, sheet metal, cardboard, and other bulky items. The primary objective in dealing with this material class is space management; dollar investment is a secondary consideration. At Hewlett-Packard, class B items represent approximately 4 percent of dollars spent and about 3 percent of part numbers. Daily delivery is also suggested for this category of parts.

CLASS C PARTS

This class consists of low dollar investment materials. The primary objective for these items is a specific performance service level. At Hewlett-Packard, 94 percent of purchased parts fall into this category, but they represent only about 8 percent of dollars spent. For materials in this category, deliveries are made twice a year, on the average.

The Hewlett-Packard example will be used to complete the description of the development cycle. In past years, Hewlett-Packard used a conventional A-B-C priority structure for managing its inventory. Implementing JIT, however, forced the firm to develop a modified approach, which it called the A/C management concept. Under the A/C concept, delivery is made daily for parts classes A and B, either for inventory or space management purposes; for class C items, delivery is made on the average two times per year, with service level being the major guideline. Once the A/C concept is implemented, procurement activities can be streamlined and proper focus placed on optimizing performance of the aggregate materials function. Table 7–1 shows the relationship between part class and the selection of parts to be purchased on a JIT basis.

With A/C reclassification the goal is zero backorders for all C parts. This strategy appears to be realistic but may well involve more frequent reviews of order points, safety stock, and so on. Further refinements of the system may include the reduction of the dollar limit for A items to bring more items under JIT management. Such action would continue to reduce inventory levels and to expand JIT purchasing responsibility.

Determining Delivery Frequency

The determination of delivery frequency in most organizations is based on an analysis that tends to minimize the sum of all incremental costs associated with or influenced by material deliveries. The Hewlett-Packard Company utilizes a relatively simple model based on this concept. The assumptions inherent in the use of the Hewlett-Packard model are:

1. The only significant incremental costs associated with delivery frequency are freight and inventory holding costs.
2. Buying costs, as well as related materials management

TABLE 7–1. Purchasing Strategy: A Framework for Selecting JIT Parts

Parts	Class A	Class B	Class C
Volume	3%	3%	94%
Dollars	88%	4%	8%
Frequency of shipment	Daily	Daily	2–4 per year
Strategy	Inventory management	Space management	Service level

Source: Hewlett-Packard Company, Greeley Division.

overhead and direct labor costs, do not vary significantly with delivery frequency.*

To use the Hewlett-Packard model, two basic calculations must be made:

1. Average daily carrying cost (ADCC) associated with a given part through the following formula:

$$\text{ADCC} = \dfrac{\left[\left(\begin{array}{c}\text{standard}\\\text{unit cost}\end{array} \times \begin{array}{c}\text{6-month}\\\text{usage}\end{array}\right) \Big/ 2\right]\left(\begin{array}{c}\text{inventory}\\\text{carrying cost}\end{array}\right)}{\dfrac{26 \text{ weeks}}{\text{frequency of delivery per week}}}$$

2. Average daily shipping cost (ADSC) associated with a given part through the following formula:

$$\text{ADSC} = \dfrac{\text{weekly freight cost}}{\text{frequency of delivery per week}}$$

Using these two values (ADCC and ADSC) along with arbitrarily selected "delivery frequency" figures (β) and their respective complementary "holding time" figures (α), the delivery frequency can be calculated by inserting these data in this equation:

$$\text{Total cost} = (\beta)\,(\text{ADCC}) + (\alpha)\,(\text{ADSC})$$

For example, if the delivery frequency per week is equal to five, ($\beta = 5$), the maximum holding time ($\alpha = 0.5$) will be equal to half a day. The objective of the Hewlett-Packard model is to determine the total cost for each of the five delivery frequency alternatives and to reveal the alternative that produces the lowest total cost.

It should be noted, however, that the model's theory is simply to minimize the two main cost ingredients—freight and inventory carrying cost. Special transportation arrangements pertaining to weight should also be factored into the equation. JIT purchasing should complement (not substitute) astute business decisions. Often managers believe that JIT deliveries equate to

*This assumption may vary in different companies, depending on the type of scheduling and purchasing systems and interfaces that a particular company uses.

"daily deliveries." The problem with equating these two is that the emphasis will be placed on "deliveries" as opposed to JIT's overall contribution to an organization's cost reduction goals.

Reducing Transportation Costs

Increasing pressure from rising transportation costs has forced the buyers' firms to evaluate their current methods of distribution and consider more cost-effective strategies. All the firms we surveyed were engaged in continuing efforts to reduce the freight cost component of the total cost structure using the following three strategies:

1. Develop an inbound freight consolidation program
2. Develop a local suppliers network
3. Develop a decentralized distribution system

Of the three strategies the first two appear to have been reasonably successful for all the firms studied. These two strategies are discussed in detail in the following paragraphs. The objective of the first strategy is to consolidate shipments of several JIT suppliers so they can share the use of a delivery vehicle, thus substantially reducing transportation costs. Although the benefits of consolidation are widely recognized, the problem with JIT consolidation programs is that they can also cause delays. Some shipments may have to wait for others to arrive to be consolidated into larger and more cost-effective shipments. Several studies indicate that the mean delivery time is increased by an average of one to three days using a consolidation program. This may not be consistent with JIT requirements and may raise questions from buyers who want to engage in true JIT purchasing.[1,2,3]

In order for consolidation to be effective, delivery schedules must be coordinated. This general approach has worked particularly well for the Buick plant located in Flint, Michigan. The density of suppliers in the Detroit area apparently minimizes the coordination problem.

The second approach involves ongoing concerted attempts to deal more extensively with or to develop local suppliers, wherever practical. In heavily industrialized areas this has worked well, although the potential difficulties are obvious when buyers' operations are located some distance from major manufacturing centers. When the geographical separation of buyers and their suppliers poses problems, the larger buyers have encouraged potential suppliers to move selected production facilities to sites nearer the buying plant.

The typical incentive for a supplier to do this is a long-term contract and the closer buyer-seller relationship that often accompanies it. Some significant successes have been noted in recent years. For example, the Hoover Company, sole supplier of truck seats to Nissan, built a new plant close to the Nissan plant in Tennessee. Hoover's objective clearly was to improve its competitiveness and to be able to meet Nissan's stringent daily delivery requirements. This of course only works when the buyer gives the supplier sufficient manufacturing volume to consume the output of an entire plant. TRI-CON, a JIT supplier to Kawasaki, was also persuaded to move its operations close to the parent company in Lincoln, so they could deliver high product quality more frequently and reduce transportation costs. The Buick Division has encouraged its suppliers to locate their plants close to "Buick City" in Flint, Michigan. In fact, this is one of the important ways suppliers can increase their chances of winning contracts with the Buick Division.[4]

SUMMARY

Most firms utilize the JIT concept of the procurement of a relatively small percentage of their total production needs, concentrating on the critical, high-value items. It appears that the additional transportation costs associated with some JIT programs are viewed by a number of purchasing and materials managers as deterrents to using the JIT purchasing approach. In actuality, a perceptive manager should be concerned with the sum of all the incremental costs associated with a JIT program. Generally speaking, the major incremental costs to be considered are shipping costs and inventory holding costs. In the firms studied, the sum of these relevant costs favored the utilization of JIT purchasing. In other words, inventory cost savings more than offset any additional transportation costs.

An attempt has been made to provide useful frameworks for (1) selecting the items to be purchased in a JIT mode, and (2) analyzing relevant costs to determine optimal delivery scheduling. These approaches, coupled with consideration of a freight consolidation program and a program for developing local suppliers, can form the foundation for an intelligent appraisal of the potential of JIT purchasing in any firm.

Another factor in implementing JIT is design of a transportation system to meet the frequent deliveries requirements. This process will be discussed in the next chapter.

CHAPTER 8

What Transportation System Facilitates Just-In-Time Purchasing?

JIT purchasing requires a transportation system designed to meet its materials delivery requirements.

SUCCESSFUL IMPLEMENTATION OF the JIT purchasing concept has been studied from three perspectives. The supplier perspective emphasizes strong relationships between buyer and seller. A study suggested that close buyer-seller relationships are critical to successful implementation of a JIT program.[1] Another study concluded: "The success of a JIT program lies in cultivating relationships with a small group of dedicated suppliers."[2]

The organizational perspective describes the changes necessary to meet JIT requirements. One study suggested that the successful implementation of JIT purchasing depends on factors in two distinct categories: human and operational. Human factors include top management's commitment and leadership, employee readiness, and labor union support. The operational factors are: a new purchasing philosophy for establishing lot sizes, number of suppliers, long-term relationships and early supplier involvement and support, efficient receiving and materials handling procedures, accurate and firm supplier scheduling, the use of standard containers, and controlled transportation systems.[3]

The third perspective is transportation. One study has suggested that the only successful JIT program is one based on a true partnership arrangement among shippers, receivers, and carriers.[4] Such a relationship has become more feasible with recent changes in the trucking industry. Prior to 1980, the trucking industry in the United States was severely regulated with many restrictions concerning who could haul what, and under what rates and rules. The industry was a tightly controlled monopoly of a few carriers in each area who operated under the Interstate Commerce Commission (ICC) with essentially the same rates for all. With the Motor Carrier Act of 1980, ICC controls were relaxed by law and government controls virtually eliminated. The ICC authorized 12,000 new truck lines and expanded the carrying authority of about 20,000 existing truck lines, with virtual freedom in setting freight rates.

These changes have worked in favor of buyer companies and have made JIT delivery requirements much more practical and feasible. With safety stocks greatly reduced and even eliminated in many firms, the role of the transportation system has become more critical. Unless appropriate transportation strategies have been developed by the buyer to meet JIT delivery requirements, the implementation of JIT will probably fail.

This chapter presents several strategies, as demonstrated in Figure 8–1, for designing a transportation system to meet these delivery requirements. First, the logistics manager should develop an organizational structure that supports every aspect of the transportation system. Second, the number of carriers should be reduced to a manageable size for control purposes. The third strategy advocates placing 100 percent of transportation services on a contract basis. The fourth strategy is the development of an extensive computer interface with all contract carriers. Fifth, all pick-up and delivery is to be on a scheduled basis. Finally, efficient materials handling techniques must be developed—for example, the standardization of pallets.

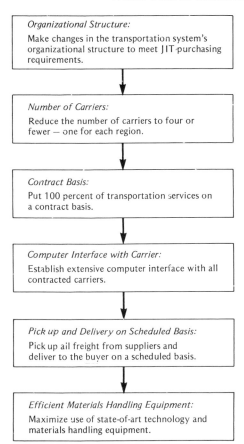

Organizational Structure:

Make changes in the transportation system's organizational structure to meet JIT purchasing requirements.

Number of Carriers:

Reduce the number of carriers to four or fewer — one for each region.

Contract Basis:

Put 100 percent of transportation services on a contract basis.

Computer Interface with Carrier:

Establish extensive computer interface with all contracted carriers.

Pick up and Delivery on Scheduled Basis:

Pick up ail freight from suppliers and deliver to the buyer on a scheduled basis.

Efficient Materials Handling Equipment:

Maximize use of state-of-art technology and materials handling equipment.

FIGURE 8-1   A Transportation System to Meet JIT Delivery Requirements

ORGANIZATIONAL STRUCTURE

Perhaps the most important strategy for a buyer company in making the transportation system work under a JIT program is to make necessary changes in organization. The logistics manager must develop close coordination among transportation, distribution, and warehousing. If this coordination is not in place before a JIT program is initiated, it cannot be implemented successfully. One department should assume the major responsibility of planning and controlling the movement of materials to, through, and out of the company. This differs from traditional practices where many independent departments, such as traffic, distribution, customer service, purchasing, and even production planning or manufacturing, have shared these responsibilities.

About 60 percent of firms responding to a survey indicated that this responsibility should be placed with the logistics manager.[3] The logistics manager, for example, should evaluate whether the existing facilities layout and materials handling system efficiently support JIT delivery requirements.[2]

With low safety stocks, the buyer's logistics department must assume new responsibilities such as knowledge of the carrier's financial statements. It is not uncommon for freight carriers to file for bankruptcy. Disruption of in-transit freight while ownership of the cargo is being determined could cause entire production lines to shut down.

Generally, profitability of truck lines is set by the industry at a 93 percent operating ratio (ratio of expenses to income), but there is considerable flexibility to go higher if the structure of the truck line is understood. With knowledge of this ratio, a buyer can avoid the bankrupt carriers and those who cannot support proper insurance and maintenance of equipment.

Other general challenges faced by the logistics manager are:

1. Identifying the people in the organization who will do the necessary planning
2. Projecting organizational requirements to meet the materials delivery needs of the firm at the start of production
3. Identifying traffic work-load changes due to conversion (from traditional to JIT) and redirecting personnel to best support firm planning
4. Identifying training needs of employees and preparing them to meet the changes

NUMBER OF CARRIERS

The second important strategy in meeting JIT materials delivery requirements is a drastic reduction in the number of carrier companies used. For a long time it has been the philosophy of many firms that competition in the transportation industry fosters the lowest cost, especially for inbound freight. For this reason, firms on average deal with 100 or more independent freight carriers.

Prior to the adoption of JIT, for example, General Motors' Buick Division purchased about $6 billion worth of commodities each year from about 600 suppliers. The commodities were delivered by more than 100 different carrier companies. Currently, the Buick Division and other companies deal with only a few carrier companies.

The drawback to using a large number of inbound freight carriers is the difficulty in maintaining complete control over each carrier. If the buyer uses a multitude of carriers, the actual per shipment cost might be lower than under the contract. But the quality of service is also lower, and working relationships under such cut-throat conditions create unnecessary tension between carriers and buyer.

Perhaps even more important is use of the buyer company's resources. The Traffic Manager at Hewlett-Packard stated that, despite a potential savings of $5,000 to $6,000 a year which a carrier company may offer, "We cannot afford to spend our resources to deal with 100 or more independent carriers as we did in the past." Cost saving on individual shipments does not compensate for the cost of managing their internal resources to deal with each individual carrier. A reduction in the number of carriers may result in substantial savings in the overall delivered cost of inbound materials.

For the traffic department to gain better control of carrier functions and thus increase operational flexibility, it is necessary to reduce the number of carriers. Seventy-eight percent of the firms that responded to a survey questionnaire indicated that they used fewer carriers after establishing JIT purchasing.[5]

The steps to follow when reducing the number of carriers are summarized as follows:

1. Select potential carriers based on their ability to meet JIT requirements. See Exhibit 8–1 for detailed criteria.
2. Develop factors for constructing freight rates. See Exhibit 8–2.
3. Split the country into regions.
4. Analyze freight volumes and origins in each region and assign carriers to each region.
5. Contact carriers regarding their selection, contingent upon factors discussed in Exhibits 8–1 and 8–2.
6. Begin negotiations of individual contracts.

CONTRACT BASIS

Another important strategy is to put 100 percent of transportation services on a contract basis. The contract is necessary not so much for restrictive and legal requirements but for assurance that operation will be conducted for a certain period of time. This is very important for both parties.

Prior to deregulation, there was less competition among air and surface carriers. Buying transportation services on a contract basis was difficult because it required a mastery of rules, regulations, and tariff tables.[6] With deregulation, significant changes in the industry's market structure have made it possible for buyers to deal with carriers on a contract basis.

The contract should be for three to five years. A one-year contract does not allow the two parties to realize the full potential of the relationship. The cost of the arrangement will take at least that long to be recovered by the supplier, given the computer, programs, and specialized equipment needed to work with the material handling system of the buyer.

Under traditional practice, carriers often failed to deliver shipments on time due to factors such as trucker strikes and transportation tie-ups. A John Fluke Manufacturing Company traffic manager said: "For so long carriers came in and said, 'I will give you three days service'; then they would not live up to their promise and nobody paid much attention."

A JIT purchasing program cannot be successful unless carriers consistently deliver their shipments on schedule. To assure this process, the buying companies must deal with the carriers on a contract basis. The result of a recent study by Lieb and Miller showed that 73 percent of firms that have implemented JIT purchasing have negotiated specific contracts with carriers to meet their JIT delivery requirements.[5] Carriers are then responsible for meeting schedules that are rigidly defined in the contract. "If a carrier shipment coming from Texas falls behind schedule, they have to fly it without bothering us with the problem," notes a Buick manager.

Penalty clauses in the contract transfer the disruption cost due to substandard carrier performance such as late shipments to the carrier. A penalty clause should not consider problems that are the result of uncontrollable circumstances and should not be used by the buyer to protect only the buyer company. Penalty clauses have been used by GM and many others in the Michigan and central state area.

To have 100 percent of transportation services on a contract basis, the following steps must be taken:

1. Institute a pilot program with selected surface and air carriers.
2. Transfer all business to the respective carriers with an understanding that
   (a) negotiation of a contract is a top priority, and
   (b) a computer interface must be developed.
3. Negotiate and sign a one-year contract with automatic renewal for up to five more years, unless reopening is desired.
4. Monitor shipments for incorrect handling and correct mis-shipments to insure the right carrier is being used.

COMPUTER INTERFACE WITH CARRIERS

An extensive computer interface with all carriers is necessary for scheduling and planning, method of payment, and tracing capability. Firms that have adopted JIT manufacturing must know when a shipment will arrive at the receiving dock. Such technology is available and is used by many surface commercial carriers. A new system developed for personal computers by Geostar Corporation—"radio-determination-satellite service"—can locate a truck in transit to within a quarter of a mile. The system has been tested successfully with a few companies. It is very inexpensive—$165 a month per truck, compared to an average cost of $24 every time a driver has to stop and call the office.[7]

Traditionally, traffic departments have "chased their tails"; that is, they have traced and expedited materials movements from each origination point. Computer interface with the carriers has helped departments to monitor the business instead of chasing the business. In addition, computer interface between the traffic department of the buyer company and the carrier can result in several mutually important benefits:

Improved Scheduling and Planning Information

Computer interfaces help carrier companies update the buyer's records as the materials move, allowing the buyer company to update its scheduling system. The system could be upgraded even more if suppliers could also be incorporated into a computerized scheduling system. With less time spent monitoring external materials flow, the buyer can concentrate on other purchasing issues. If the flow of materials can be scheduled in advance, the transportation company will be better equipped to plan the pickup and delivery schedules, which should result in a lower percentage of late deliveries. This system will work if complete and accurate disclosure of information is available to both parties. The computer interface also provides the capability of pulling together information to analyze the cost-effectiveness and service performance of the carrier. Achieving on-time deliveries is one of the most important benefits of using information technology.[5]

An Efficient and Accurate Method of Payment

Since shipment rates are prenegotiated, buyer companies know exactly what each shipment costs, how much carrier companies have shipped, and how much they have received. The buyer companies can immediately pay the exact amount electronically to the carriers. This puts much of the responsibility of auditing back on the carrier. The companies studied agreed that buyer companies should no longer be in the auditing mode and it is the carriers' responsibility to see that the amount paid to them is correct.

Less Paperwork

Preparing and processing shipping documents and invoices and making the necessary changes in the delivery schedules demand significant amounts of time and paperwork. Computer integration of scheduling can drastically reduce the paperwork load for both buyer and carrier, creating a system that is both efficient and effective. This benefit has been cited elsewhere.[5]

Following are some of the factors that require careful attention in defining and developing the computer interface requirements:

FOR THE BUYER COMPANY:

1. Capability of transmitting and receiving freight payment electronically
2. Ability to quickly reach top account management for problem solving and to handle emergencies
3. Capability of monitoring the location of any shipment at any time
4. Availability of historical data to analyze carriers' service performance

FOR THE CARRIER COMPANY:

1. Systems in place to facilitate monitoring all the buyer's shipments
2. Dedication of one person to the buyer company to problem-solve and handle emergencies

PICK-UP AND DELIVERY
ON SCHEDULED BASIS

If JIT purchasing is to be effective, all freight must be picked up and delivered on a scheduled basis. In the past, due in part to carrier regulation, many companies left the scheduling and handling of inbound freight to the supplier or to the carrier company, regardless of whether the purchase contract stated free on board (FOB) destination or FOB origin. Traffic departments did not concentrate on inbound freight because their success was measured in terms of lowering outbound freight costs.

In traditional practice, delivery scheduling gave the carrier company "freedom of the week," that is, within a given week, the carrier could ship the lot on whichever day worked most economically for the carrier. Under this practice, it was impossible to meet on-time materials delivery.

The result was excess inventory. The buyer needed to have five days' inventory on hand because the carrier might deliver the shipment as late as Friday. If the buyer expected delivery on Wednesday and the shipment arrived on Friday, the buyer would run out of inventory. If the carrier shipped parts on Monday, however, the buyer had to carry five extra days' worth of inventory.

One way to eliminate, or at least minimize, this problem is to give the carriers the pick-up dates and times scheduled from the supplier and the delivery dates and times scheduled to the buyer's receiving docks. The carrier then proposes a schedule that will satisfy service requirements and minimize carrier costs. Once the carrier and the buyer's traffic department agree on a schedule, it becomes part of the contract.

The key factor in successfully implementing this strategy is the extensive training and education of the carrier in the buyer company's overall objectives. The sequence of steps is as follows:

1. Specify suppliers
2. Work with the carriers to agree on a pick-up schedule from the suppliers
3. Schedule deliveries to the buyer
4. Identify which carriers have delivered
5. Schedule return of suppliers' empty racks and containers

EFFICIENT AND STANDARDIZED MATERIALS HANDLING EQUIPMENT

Efficient handling of materials requires state-of-the-art technology in packaging and equipment at the buyer's receiving docks. With regard to packaging, there is a general movement among U.S. companies who have adopted the concept of JIT purchasing to eliminate traditional methods (e.g., corrugated packs and cardboard boxes) and adopt standard packaging. The Buick Division has designed trailers for the Detroit area to optimize space and meet JIT requirements as described in Chapter 5.

Sophisticated flow-through terminal systems at the buyer's receiving areas should be integrated to smooth and efficient materials movement throughout the plant. Since standard containers are used to deliver parts, each container should have a bar code. Laser scanners can then monitor materials at the receiving points and as they move through the system. As a result, the buyer knows exactly the location and quantity of materials on hand at all times.

Materials handling can also be facilitated by:

1. Identifying parts for potential specialized equipment delivery
2. Working with contract carriers to obtain appropriate equipment, such as tautliners, roller equipped floors, and removable shelves
3. Developing equipment to be used for JIT delivery from the supplier to the buyer's point-of-use docks
4. Designing a flow-through terminal to incorporate extensive use of automated materials handling equipment, such as a computerized stocker and bar code readers for receiving
5. Standardizing the pallet system

SUMMARY

The corporate transportation system plays a major role in the successful implementation of JIT purchasing. Firms using JIT purchasing can also expect a financial payoff from the transportation system in terms of lower inventories, reduced warehouse expenses, improved product quality and productivity, and decreased administrative costs.

This chapter has suggested several strategies for meeting JIT materials delivery requirements. The most important strategy is to have an appropriate transportation organizational structure in place prior to initiation of JIT purchasing. The second strategy is to reduce the number of carriers to a manageable number in order to gain better control over them and a more efficient use of the buyer's resources. Third, sign one-year contracts with potential carriers for 100 percent services (pick-up and delivery) and apply penalty clauses for late shipments. Fourth, develop an extensive computer interface system with all contract carriers to improve scheduling, planning information, and method of payment, and to reduce paperwork. Fifth, assign to each carrier a pick-up time schedule from the supplier and a delivery time schedule to the receiving docks to assure on-time delivery and reduce excess inventory. The sixth strategy is to maximize the use of state-of-the-art technology in packaging and materials handling equipment. When all these strategies are developed and implemented, the transportation system will be in a position to facilitate and support JIT purchasing.

EXHIBIT 8–1   Carrier Selection for Just-In-Time Delivery Requirements

A. *General overview of carrier selection*
   1. Must be profitable, 93% operating ratio or better.
   2. Must have a fallback facility near the buyer's plant.
   3. Must have proper cargo and liability insurance.
   4. Must have proper and sufficient trucking equipment.
B. *Less-than-truckload (LTL) carrier selection*
   1. Must have a terminal close to the buyer's plant so buyers do not get delayed shipments.
   2. Normal service time must be published and evaluated against actual performance.
   3. Rates must be fair and meet the JIT conditions. Bids should go out to preselected LTL carriers who can do the job.
C. *Truckload carrier selection*
   1. Carriers must have a base in or near supplier locations.
   2. Truckload rates should be put out for bid to preselected truckers. Point-to-point truckload rates should be sought.

EXHIBIT 8–2   Factors for Constructing Freight Rates

A. *Delivery dependability*
   1. Assure dependability first by getting a good carrier.
   2. Guarantee a delivery penalty.
   3. Protect against loss and damage claims.
   4. Provide liability insurance for cargo and public losses.
   5. Guarantee return of empty racks and containers.
   6. Ensure good condition of the shipment.
   7. Implement an efficient system of tracing and expediting.
B. *Rate level negotiation (with above conditions)*
   1. *Less-than-truckload rates*
      a. A percentage discount from the standard tariff charges
      b. A point-to-point specific "commodity" rate from the suppliers to the buyer's plant
   2. *Truckload rates*
      a. On a mileage basis if round-trip mileage is involved
      b. On a point-to-point specified "commodity" rate for the movement involved

CHAPTER 9

How Does JIT Purchasing Improve Product Quality and Productivity?

In U.S. firms, JIT purchasing can be a "quality and productivity center."

IN THE EARLY 1960s, the purchasing function was treated as a "cost center" whose performance was measured by other departments' satisfaction. Its primary functions and responsibilities within manufacturing firms included such tasks as preparing and processing invoices and purchase orders, receiving items, making payment, and other low level activities.

In the late 1960s and early 1970s, however, many companies realized that profits could be improved by developing a purchasing system that was treated as a "profit center," rather than a cost center. Ammer explains that when the materials department transfers material to manufacturing at a price that is normally greater than its total allocated costs, it is functioning as a profit center.[1] During this profit center period, purchasing's major functions and responsibilities grew to include vendor analysis, sources evaluation, purchasing policy, corporate planning, new product planning, and others.

From the mid-1970s on, many manufacturing firms began to experience new problems in purchasing vital materials due to the oil embargo, shortages of some raw materials, high interest rates, a period of double-digit inflation, and longer lead times. These problems forced manufacturing firms to think about "hand-to-mouth" stockholding policies. This term is actually equivalent to the Japanese concept of just-in-time.[2]

As a result, many U.S. manufacturing firms have recognized that purchasing activities are as important to the success of the firm as areas of finance, marketing, engineering, personnel, production control, and quality control. One indication that purchasing functions have grown in importance is a report by the U.S. Department of Commerce's Census of Manufacturing for 1988 that service costs for purchasing account for 57.8 percent of the total cost of manufacturing.

Although several propositions, such as adopting total quality control concepts and massive quality training, have been offered by experts for quality improvement in the 1980s, there has been no emphasis on the function of purchasing. Yet product quality and productivity can be improved through successful implementation of the JIT purchasing concept. Therefore, we propose that JIT purchasing be treated as a "quality and productivity center."

How do quality and productivity relate to purchasing? A great deal of confusion exists about productivity measurement because it has different meanings for different individuals. To production workers, productivity is associated with their work efforts—for example, the number of wires they connect per day. To the plant manager, productivity is equal to total output, such as the number of motorcycles workers can assemble per day. The executive focuses on the profitability of the plant, while the purchasing department is concerned with the quality of parts delivered and the efficiency with which resources are used to produce final goods for the marketplace. All these different views, however, associate productivity with the ratio of output (measure of product in physical volume, profit, or added value) to input (such as manpower, materials, machinery, and capital).

The greater the disparity between input and output through higher product quality, the greater the productivity. The traditional view shared by many suppliers has been that the achievement of higher quality requires greater cost and does not lead to higher productivity. Crosby directly challenges this relationship, proposing that lower quality will decrease productivity due to the increased cost of manufacturing a higher failure rate. Such a rate requires more raw material, higher machine downtime, increased inspection time, and higher labor time.[3]

According to the Committee for Economic Development, since failure rate is a significant element of quality, quality is literally an important component of productivity. All other factors being constant (such as capital and manpower), the lower a firm's failure rate, the less their inputs are wasted and the greater their productivity.

The JIT purchasing system deals with both factors, the failure rate and waste. The aim of this chapter is to identify the major activities of JIT purchasing practices that have favorable effects on product quality and productivity in U.S. firms and to describe how these effects have improved product quality and productivity.

WHAT ARE THE MAJOR ACTIVITIES OF JIT PURCHASING THAT IMPROVE QUALITY AND PRODUCTIVITY?

Through our discussions with purchasing, quality control, production, engineering and design, and transportation and traffic managers, eight major activities of JIT purchasing that are generally considered important in improving product quality and productivity were identified, as demonstrated in Table 9–1. These discussions revealed several important points.[4] First, all the managers agreed that the list in Table 9–1 represents the major activities of JIT purchasing. Second, all managers indicated that important relationships exist between these activities and improving quality and productivity in their companies. Third, all the managers evaluated the average relative importance of the activities similarly.

The managers indicated that purchase lot-size, number of suppliers, supplier selection and evaluation, quality inspection, the bidding process, and design specifications are *very important* in improving product quality and productivity. Paperwork was

TABLE 9–1. Major Activities of JIT Purchasing in Improving Product Quality and Productivity

Activity	Characteristics
1. Purchase lot size	Exact quantities in small lot-sizes
2. Number of suppliers	Fewer in number—ideally one for each material or class of parts
3. Supplier selection and evaluation	Based on quality, mutual relationships, delivery performance, etc.
4. Quality inspection	Performed at suppliers' plants
5. Design specifications	More freedom given to suppliers to meet design specifications
6. Bidding	Stay with same suppliers, no annual rebidding
7. Paperwork	Informal paperwork
8. Packaging	Standard containers and rack utilized

considered *important* by all involved managers. Packaging was the only activity that was ranked lower, as *fairly important*.

Our studies show that product quality and productivity have improved substantially because of JIT purchasing. A study conducted by C. O'Neal among 23 different companies also has reached the same conclusion.[5] The effect of JIT purchasing activities seems to vary according to the extent and length of time that the firm has implemented the JIT concept. Most results are difficult to measure with precision. The effect of purchase lot sizes, for example, could be significant or insignificant, depending on factors such as the degree of change in lot size, the frequency of delivery, the suppliers' efforts, the type of product, skill levels of the employees, and so on. The following sections describe how managers perceive JIT purchasing activities as improving product quality and productivity.

Purchase Lot Size

Probably the most important single method of improving product quality and productivity is to buy parts in small lot sizes. The smaller the lot size, the easier it is to inspect the lot and uncover defects or flaws immediately. Parts that are purchased steadily in small lot sizes with frequent deliveries (daily or weekly) contribute to higher productivity through lower levels of inventory and scrap, high product quality, lower inspection costs for incoming parts, and an early detection of defects.

However, some potentially serious issues have been raised relating to the desirability of frequent (daily or weekly) deliveries for each and every part. No hard and fast rules apply. For instance, at the Hewlett-Packard Greeley Division, more than 4,000 part numbers are purchased, but only a few (about 45) are delivered on a JIT basis. The reasons are:

1. It makes little sense for a company to waste its time dealing with hundreds of suppliers and purchasing thousands of part numbers on a daily/weekly basis when these activities do not result in significant benefits.
2. Common sense and practical business judgment may dictate that monthly or even yearly deliveries are in order (e.g., when an obsolete technology results in a "last chance" buy).

An issue related to lot size is freight cost. A misconception exists that daily delivery increases the cost of freight beyond the savings realized in reducing inventory. Several approaches to reducing the shipping costs associated with frequent delivery were suggested in Chapter 7. In general, small lot size has a big impact on product quality and productivity, but each company must adapt the principle in ways that meet its own needs.

Number of Suppliers

Under JIT purchasing, buyers are encouraged to buy from a small number of suppliers, ideally one for each material or class of materials. In recent years, many U.S. firms have done this and established mutually beneficial, long-term relationships.

At the time of this research, Hewlett-Packard had about 220 suppliers, one or two sources of supply for each type of part. At Kawasaki, the purchasing manager explained that for parts imported from Japan there is a single source of supply; for U.S. parts there are usually two to three suppliers. Nissan has 80 U.S. suppliers, 40 of which supply components on a JIT single source of supply basis; the remaining suppliers provide materials in large quantities. The Buick Division had about 600 suppliers. Approximately 85 are JIT suppliers, representing more than 70 percent of the expenditures.

In discussions with senior buyers or in the survey responses received from other managers, it became clear that dealing with a smaller number of supply sources has resulted in some important advantages:

1. *Long-term relationships.* With long-term relationships, buyers can work closely with suppliers and encourage them to participate fully in JIT programs. At the same time, suppliers are more willing to participate in improving product quality and increasing their capital investment. This mutual cooperation will increase the continuous supply of parts to the buyer's plant, reduce or minimize inventories, and eliminate routine paperwork.
2. *Consistent quality.* When buyers deal with fewer suppliers and involve them in the early stages of program design, the suppliers can provide consistently high quality products.
3. *Conserving resources.* With a limited number of suppliers, a minimum investment of resources such as buyer's time, travel, and engineering are required. Money can, therefore, be concentrated on selecting, developing, and monitoring one or a few qualified sources.
4. *Lower costs.* The overall volume of items purchased from each supplier is higher, which eventually leads to lower costs.
5. *Special attention.* The suppliers are more inclined to give special consideration to buyers, since the buyers represent large accounts. Buyers can rely on the suppliers' area of expertise.
6. *Savings on tooling.* The amount spent to provide tooling to the suppliers is minimal with only one source of supply.

Supplier Selection and Evaluation

The third important activity of JIT purchasing is establishment of formal supplier selection and evaluation programs. Such programs are commonplace in U.S. industry. The type of process required for accurate monitoring of the important aspects of a supplier's performance clearly varies with the complexity and dollar value of the material purchased. The following criteria are generally used for selecting and evaluating suppliers' capabilities:

1. Product quality
2. Long-term mutual relationships and cooperation
3. Delivery performance
4. Geographical location of supply source
5. Price structure

The first two factors are considered foremost. Long-term relationships shape the suppliers' attitudes and encourage them to meet the buyer's quality standards. The suppliers feel they are part of the buyer's company and that their success depends upon their buyer's success. Currently, many firms—including Hewlett-Packard, Nissan, Kawasaki, Sony, Honda, Goodyear, the Buick Division, and others—have given long-term flexible contracts to their qualified suppliers. Hewlett-Packard, for instance, has given its suppliers 18-to-36 month contracts, with the potential for renegotiation every 6 to 12 months in exchange for quality improvement and cost reduction.

The selection and evaluation of suppliers' abilities in delivery performance are based on the following factors:

1. Delivery of a high quality product
2. On time delivery
3. Frequent deliveries
4. Delivery of small quantities
5. Delivery of exact quantities

General Motors, for example, rates its suppliers by means of a numerical index based largely on quality. Ford has developed a preferred supplier list based on consistently high quality and delivery performance. All these factors are equally important and necessary in assessing delivery performance. If these criteria are met, the suppliers are considered to be qualified JIT supply sources.

Another important criterion is the geographical location of supply sources. A local supplier is preferred, but if that is not possible, the closest supply sources are usually given preference. Buyers encourage potential nonlocal suppliers to locate their operations close by. This not only reduces transportation costs but also creates opportunities for buyers, engineers, quality control people, and even production people to work closely with their suppliers in the areas of design and quality.

A competitive price structure can be a factor, but many managers agreed that low price is no longer an important criterion in selecting and evaluating suppliers. Managers are more concerned with negotiating and developing price structures that are "fair" to both parties. Low, competitive prices may have disadvantages:

1. Manufacturing losses due to poor quality
2. Higher cost of defective parts
3. More travel and other expenses associated with resolving quality problems
4. Additional costs for paperwork, packing, handling, return shipping, etc.

Quality Inspection

The fourth important JIT purchasing activity is quality inspection. Formal receipts, piece counts, identification, and general inspection of all incoming inbound freight must be eliminated at the buying company. In other words, quality control must be performed at the source by the supplier.

One method to assure the delivery of high product quality is supplier certification. When the buyer has established a long-term relationship with a supplier and has found that product quality is consistently reliable, it makes sense to leave the responsibility of inspection to the supplier. Supplier quality certification programs assure that specifications have been met before parts leave the suppliers' plants; suppliers take "ownership" of the quality requirements of parts they deliver. To help suppliers establish these programs the buyer takes an active role in training them on different aspects of SQC techniques. SQC needs of suppliers are discussed in detail in Chapter 10.

Another method effective in helping suppliers deliver high product quality is regular auditing of suppliers' plants. It is not uncommon for these audits to occur several times a year, without much advance notice. The audit group typically consists of buyers, engineers, and quality control personnel. For example, at

Boeing quality control people regularly interact with their local suppliers to improve quality and reduce cost.

Moving the responsibility for incoming parts inspection to the suppliers motivates them to achieve higher quality. Suppliers attempt to deliver high product quality to avoid additional costs. They know they must pay for defective parts produced. They also want to avoid risking possible termination of contracts. Generally, suppliers realize that under the JIT system buyers cannot be skeptical about quality matters or contracts will be terminated.

Design Specifications

Early involvement by suppliers in the development of design specifications is important. Although the design engineers hold primary responsibility for developing and for the functional performance of the material specifications, the suppliers are free to make recommendations and innovations and to discuss problems of design and quality. Specifications can thus be "loose," the buyer relying more on limited performance specifications and less on narrowly defined design specifications. Clearly, this provides more latitude for the supplier and permits more innovation in developing cost-effective solutions to the quality/function aspect of the purchase.

Early supplier involvement in design development and the availability of supplier technical knowledge throughout the entire process ensures that parts can be produced without drastic changes in tooling. For example, the purchasing manager at Hewlett-Packard noted that in the past, specifications were passed on to the suppliers, who were expected to comply with them exactly. In many instances, new tooling and drastic retooling were required to produce parts that would meet exact specifications. Under the loose specifications approach, new tooling is required less frequently (except for some critical items), thus reducing the costs of tooling and bidding.

Second, technical assistance from suppliers in the design process can ensure and upgrade the quality of parts produced; any quality problems due to tight or vague specifications are reviewed and worked out by both the purchaser and the supplier. Under this approach, the suppliers have an incentive to perfect quality.

Bidding

Many purchasing departments have established new policies and guidelines for buyers in handling the bidding process with potential JIT suppliers. The lowest qualified bidders will not necessarily get the contracts; rather, suppliers who can provide consistently high product quality with no incoming inspection, deliver on time, work with the buyer to solve problems, and provide fair pricing have the best chance to get contracts. As mentioned earlier, JIT bidding specifications are not as rigid as in traditional systems, and suppliers are encouraged to be innovative in meeting buyers' specified needs.

When a JIT purchase agreement is negotiated, the potential supplier receives the buyer's engineering drawings (with loose specifications) and responds with a bid price. Usually the buyer visits the supplier's plant to do an informal ("on the fly") value analysis. The objective is to find the suppliers' areas of high cost and help them reduce those costs over a period of time by adjusting specifications.

As a result of long-term relationships and cooperation between buyers and suppliers, the bidding process has been drastically changed. The buyers provide potential suppliers with blueprints before bids are made. Prices are occasionally adjusted by the buyer to reduce the bid price, so the supplier can save money. Once a supplier is selected, there is no need to go through annual competitive rebidding. Contracts are renegotiable annually, however.

For example, the purchasing manager at Buick Division reported that about one-half of their 85 major suppliers have been working with the Buick Division for more than thirty years. It is unnecessary to have these suppliers go through a rebidding process every year in an effort to shave a few dollars off the unit price. At other firms, potential JIT suppliers are given long-term (up to 36-month) contracts which are open to renegotiation.

Paperwork

A reduction in the amount of paperwork can contribute to improved product quality and productivity. All the managers involved in the study agreed that purchasing on a JIT basis reduces the paperwork volume and saves time for the purchasing people.

This is achieved by using long-term contracts instead of multiple purchase orders; a simple phone call can then change delivery timing or quantity levels, and kanban systems replace purchase orders. A fully implemented kanban system should greatly reduce paperwork volume.

Purchasing people thus save both buying time and delivery time. Less formal paperwork means that purchasing personnel spend less time issuing purchase orders, purchase requisitions, packing lists, shipping documents, and invoices. As a result, they have more time to audit supplier performance and cooperate in design and quality improvement. The companies surveyed feel they have not yet realized the full benefits from this activity.

Packaging

There is a general movement among U.S. companies converting to JIT purchasing to eliminate traditional packaging methods (e.g., corrugated packs, cardboard boxes, etc.) and adopt new standard containers, which hold small and precise quantities of every part number. The utilization of standard containers has great potential benefits:

1. Easy identification of precise quantities and specification of the part number
2. The facilitation of receiving and materials handling procedures, which prevents mistakes and results in less need for manpower
3. Elimination of potential damage to the parts in and out of plants
4. Reduction of packaging costs
5. Reduction of waste, resulting in cleaner work areas and saved space

The use of standard containers can influence product quality and productivity. The production manager at Buick Division found that the use of standard containers generated a positive attitude among workers. Workers pay more attention when they can see just a few parts left and are more likely to try to put them on right. The use of standard containers encourages workers to be more conscientious. Instead of the attitude that "the company has a lot of money; if we lose a part it doesn't matter," workers will pick up a dropped part because they see that the supply is limited.

Work areas are thus cleaner, neater, and less distracting, which helps workers to be careful.

SUMMARY

U.S. manufacturing firms should treat JIT purchasing as a "quality and productivity center." The results of our study indicate that quality inspection at the source of supply, small lot sizes with frequent deliveries, a drastically reduced number of suppliers, and evaluation and selection of suppliers based on quality and mutual relationships are major activities of JIT purchasing and have contributed significantly to the improvement of product quality and productivity. Supplier freedom to meet design specifications and bidding procedures through loose specifications is also considered an important effect of JIT purchasing. Paperwork and packaging have not yet contributed to the improvement of quality and productivity as fully as expected, probably because the JIT purchasing concept has not been fully implemented in suppliers' plants, and buyers have not required suppliers to utilize standard containers for delivery.

The effects of all these activities on product quality and productivity vary according to the extent and length of time the company has implemented JIT. Regardless of the company's size, the type of product, process, or manufacturing, JIT purchasing can improve product quality and productivity in U.S. firms.

CHAPTER 10

What Is the Role of Quality Control in JIT Purchasing?

A permanent quality program is necessary for suppliers' commitment to quality excellence

SO FAR WE HAVE EMPHASIZED that the success of a JIT purchasing program relies heavily on consistent high product quality delivered, and have not stressed responsibility for quality. In many firms a controversy exists about who is responsible for product quality—buyers or suppliers? Usually suppliers are held responsible. However, properly organized quality programs do not always exist in supplier companies. To overcome this problem, it has become common practice in recent years for buyers to summon their suppliers, give them one-time fundamental quality control training, and follow up with questionnaires or requests for control charts. Although this may be better than no action, it does not encourage suppliers to make a commitment to consistently excellent quality.

To fulfill this commitment, a permanent quality program is required for suppliers' operations, with constant communication between buyer and supplier. The program should start with a strategic plan that emphasizes integration of quality control (QC) techniques with every supplier's manufacturing activities. This requires ongoing training of their work forces, including executives, managers, and salaried and hourly employees. Training in QC techniques includes how they may be applied effectively and be then reinforced for quality excellence.

Therefore, this chapter discusses the development of strategic quality plans, reviews QC programs and their essential techniques, examines reasons for slow implementation, and details benefits obtained from establishing QC programs.

DEVELOPING A STRATEGIC QUALITY PLAN

A strategic quality plan centers on the supplier's goal of bringing world-class quality to every product line within the company and doing it in such a way that improvement is a never-ending discipline. This goal creates a challenging environment for management. Annual quality plans encompass all disciplines of the company:

- preventing defects rather than detecting them
- integrating quality control programs with all operating disciplines of design, manufacturing, and logistics
- assigning the responsibility of quality control to operating departments
- building the continuing quality improvement programs into capital and operating plans
- establishing a quality measurement and reporting system with appropriate details for management and employee information
- establishing individual quality performance as part of the formal personnel evaluation program
- providing continuous communication with buyers for clear understanding of their requirements

The strategic quality plan developed by Honda Motor Company for its suppliers is an excellent example. It has been structured so that development of the plan and training for all levels of the organization proceed concurrently. This helps improve standards; information generated becomes the basis for analytical troubleshooting, and, therefore, a permanent part of their operations.

A strategic quality plan also places a special importance on raising the level of commitment for group problem solving. Employees and operating personnel are trained and motivated together to recognize their primary job: relentless daily pursuit of quality improvement. At Hewlett-Packard, for example, the quality program stresses training managers at different levels of the organization to train their subordinates. The program requires a commitment by both management and the production work force. This commitment is clear in the internal training division staffed by employees of the industrial relations division. The training provided by this division maintains continuity and helps improve the management-union relationship, while recognizing the beneficial effects of training on quality.

A strategic quality plan stresses two criteria: (1) QC techniques learned through training must be applicable, and (2) they must be reinforced. A good example is at LTV Steel where the QC techniques taught are clearly applied to different operations and trained personnel integrate the new techniques into their day-to-day activities and with the complete support of their immediate superiors. Training the task force is considered an ongoing process with the constant contribution of buyers. This requires continuous reviewing of their existing procedures, building in buyers' requirements, and applying QC techniques for quality excellence.

WHAT MAKES A GOOD QUALITY CONTROL PROGRAM?

Quality control programs in suppliers' companies must integrate all aspects of product quality: design, to meet the buyer's requirements; production, to meet the full intent of the buyer's specifications; and inspection, to determine whether the resulting product conforms to specifications and is shipped safely to buyers. Based on these requirements, we propose a comprehensive quality control approach to suppliers for obtaining quality excellence (Figure 10–1).

This approach gives high priority to two factors: first, obtaining quality excellence through the implementation of quality con-

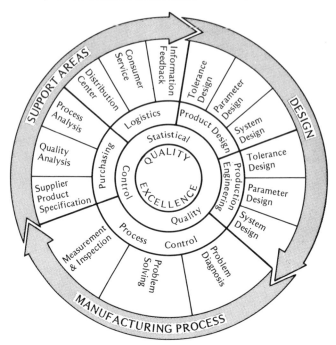

FIGURE 10–1   Comprehensive Approach to Quality Excellence

trol techniques with the participation of top management, employees, and production personnel throughout the entire system; second, identifying problems and taking corrective actions at every manufacturing activity and providing ongoing feedback to other activities. QC activities as presented in Table 10–1 are divided into three areas: design control, manufacturing process control, and logistics (quality control for distribution centers and consumer services).

Design Control

QC in engineering design helps suppliers achieve several design objectives (such as product reliability, safety, and functional features) while developing a product. The use of QC in design thus helps suppliers develop a trouble-free product. QC provides for the optimization of design elements, and assures that the design is robust enough to perform satisfactorily, with little or no harmful side effects, for the lifetime of the product. QC also helps suppli-

TABLE 10–1. Quality Control Activities

Activity	Description	Process
Design control	Product design	Product system design
		Product parameter design
		Product tolerance design
	Production engineering	Process system design
		Process parameter design
		Process tolerance design
Manufacturing process control	Diagnosis and problem solving	Defining problems
		Identifying control variables
		Identifying causes
		Analyzing causes
		Drawing conclusions
		Developing and improving standards
		Implementing actions
		Analyzing goals
	Purchasing	
Logistics quality control		Distribution centers
		Consumer services

ers make the product easy to manufacture and insensitive to variability on the factory floor.

These objectives can be obtained by controlling quality in the stages of product design and production engineering before the product goes into full-scale production.

PRODUCT DESIGN

Product quality and determination of the variations of product performance under different conditions are defined in a three-step approach during the design and R&D phases: product system design, product parameter design, and product tolerance design. This three-step design is known as the Taguchi Method.[1] Although based upon conventional experimental design, the Taguchi Method makes some radical departures from statistical methods commonly used in the United States by adding parameter design to the design process.

1. *Product system design* involves the basic design and testing of all parts and components for a desired product perfor-

mance, utilizing knowledge from specialized fields. In designing a TV power circuit, for example, an electrical engineer's knowledge is needed to design an electronic circuit that will convert a 100-volt alternating current into a 115-volt direct current. Once the system design is completed, the target specification (mean) of the factors comprised by the product component is defined.

Most suppliers consider system design the principal design process and use classical statistical techniques (such as regression or randomized design) during this phase. The use of classical statistics, however, does not help them to optimize the level of components nor does it show the effect of unknown factors on known factors.

2. *Product parameter design* is the determination of the level of each component that will infuse the least variation into the product performance. At this stage, design engineers attempt to optimize the level of parameters (or components) so that their variation due to controllable or uncontrolled factors has a minimum impact on product performance.

In the parameter design phase, it is important for suppliers and engineers to realize that the desired product performance may change due to known or controllable factors in the design, such as dimensions of product components and interactions among them, and unknown or uncontrollable factors, such as humidity, temperature, product deterioration, and possible abuse of product by the buyer.

From a quality standpoint, parameter design is the most important aspect of design in developing a trouble-free product. At this stage, optimization is applied to find the average (mean) level of components or to discover the combination of component levels that is capable of damping the influence of controllable and uncontrollable factors.

With completion of parameter design, the system is at its highest level of performance with the lowest possible costs. The resulting product is compared with its design specifications as defined in system design before it is developed further.

3. *Product tolerance design* is the final stage of the design process. Tolerance design is considered only if product performance is not acceptable at the parameter design stage. It determines how much variation from the target specification can be allowed, taking cost and product performance into account. The components that perform well over a wide range of tolerance are

less apt to cause problems during usage. If a wide range is not possible, then optimization of components will be considered— that is, which component parts should be of higher quality (more expensive) and which ones may have lower quality (less expensive).

If the product performance is not satisfactory following the initial system design, the next step for some suppliers is upgrading materials and tightening of tolerance. Their designers simply replace components that fail with more expensive ones, without optimizing those components. The final design released for manufacturing, therefore, exceeds the original budgeted costs and increases expenses extensively.

PRODUCTION ENGINEERING

After the completion of product design, a production process is designed with the objective of providing uniform products economically. The process has the same three steps as product design: system, parameter, and tolerance design.

1. *Process system design* specifies manufacturing processes and their connecting systems.

2. *Process parameter design* involves diminishing the influence of various uncontrollable factors in production processes. For example, in a tile-baking process, the dimensions of baked tiles are not uniform because temperatures vary at different spots in a tunnel kiln. An experiment showed that adding 5 percent of one kind of lime to the original compound diminishes the temperature effect on the tiles by 90 percent.[2] This is the only method known to produce higher product quality without increasing costs.

3. *Process tolerance design* improves the equipment or decreases the causes of errors. It is often not economical, however, to remove causes entirely. Therefore, sensitivity to variations should be minimized in parameter design for product and process design.

Both product design and production engineering are enhanced by using *signal-to-noise ratio*. This S/N ratio allows analysis of independent factors that cause variability in product performance. It demonstrates how some factors have an effect on changing the mean, while others will affect variability. The role of factors affecting variability cannot be determined using conventional statistics.

S/N ratio also has a unique application in evaluating test equipment used to manufacture uniform components and to narrow the tolerance of components. Manufacturing a uniform product requires an accurate means of measuring without distortion or error. For example, designers at Goodyear indicated that measuring and adjusting the dimensions of an extruded piece of hose is important for making immediate adjustments to the extrusion rate and maintaining hose wall thickness. A good piece of test equipment must be sensitive with small measuring error. It would be useless if the sensitivity were improved at the cost of a large error of measurement.

Manufacturing Process Control

With the completion of product and process design the product is sent for full-scale production. During production, quality of product varies with variations in raw materials, work methods, measurements, or equipment. This variation necessitates QC activity concentrated in the routine manufacturing operations, an activity identified by many suppliers as manufacturing process control.

Manufacturing process control relates to design control through two phases of diagnosis and problem-solving. The object is to maintain process and product specifications according to the designed standards and to ensure production of uniform products. These objectives can be obtained by diagnosing and solving the problems within the production process.

DIAGNOSIS AND PROBLEM SOLVING

Diagnosis and problem solving constitute a method of logically analyzing process data to arrive at a decision on process control. It includes QC techniques to determine and improve the effectiveness of product and process standards. If the process is capable of producing the product according to established standards, then production continues without any improving operations. If not, additional QC information, such as control charts, is needed to diagnose and solve the problem.

Once this information is obtained, testing the effectiveness of a product standard continues with testing the process. Hewlett-Packard, for example, uses a computer program that keeps track of the number of units that have failed and, based upon the determined control limits, instructs the operator to count and plot the number of failed units in any sample on the chart kept at the operator's position. If the number of failures in a sample exceeds the limit, the program stops all testing operations and instructs the operator to take corrective action.

At LTV Steel, diagnosis and problem solving consists of nine steps that reinforce logical analysis from the beginning of the manufacturing process. These steps are explained briefly here.

1. *Defining process.* The process flow chart is the primary tool for process definition. It is a pictorial representation of the process constructed by listing and relating all the steps of production in sequential order. Once the process is defined, analysis is conducted to find quality-related problems.

2. *Defining problems.* QC decisions stress problem definition at different steps of production as the primary step for suppliers in problem solving. At Boeing Aerospace Company, for example, operations problems are defined as deviation of behavior or events from design requirements or the buyer's specifications.

3. *Identifying control variables.* Identification of key variables is an essential part of diagnosis. At this stage, data is collected and a process control map is developed to identify those variables having a significant effect on quality and/or other related manufacturing disciplines. The process control map has several secondary purposes: improving a numbering system for identifying variables; presenting a clear picture of how each key variable fits into the overall process; and monitoring the system's progress.

The process control map highlights three fundamental areas: control areas, control points, and control elements. The control area is a physical location with definite, logical boundaries and with some or all of the following attributes: a single, well-defined, overall task performed at the area; a clearly assigned work force; and output that is specifically measurable in terms of quality. A control area covers a relatively large section of a department's operation and encompasses a number of significant activities. These activities are the control points.

Control elements are subdivisions of control points. They must be objective and fall within two general categories: numerical measurements, such as temperature or pressure, and attributes that clearly describe issues, such as sequence of operations or maintenance. For example, raw material (which includes materials handling, supplier packaging requirements, storage practices, etc.) is a control area. Testing incoming materials is a control point, and scrap is a control element.

4. *Identifying causes.* Once the control variables have been identified, the next step is to identify causes of unacceptable quality and relate them to control variables in a complex production process. This requires identifying the most likely causes and eliminating unlikely causes.

5. *Analyzing causes.* An analysis of each probable cause is based on collected data and involves statistical analysis of the data.

6. *Drawing conclusions.* Drawing a conclusion follows readily from the preceding steps, but the conclusion must also be based on other information (such as past experience, lab experiments, and group brainstorming). Any conclusion reached must be supported by the analysis in the previous step and verified with new data.

7. *Developing/improving standards.* Every conclusion that leads to a new decision for improvement must be addressed in great detail in a standardized format. Developing standards necessitates revising the existing procedure, building in the buyer's requirements, and controlling new standards.

Controlling new standards includes control of the following: process standard definitions, product standards definitions, measurement and routine reporting of products, and operating procedures using process capability studies.

Upon review and approval by buyers, design engineers, and QC managers, a new standard is issued which leads to higher product quality. For example, based on statistical analysis of a 1982 study at LTV Steel, a significant reduction in bloom cracks was achieved by increasing the minimum skin temperature to 1500 degrees. The result was supported by a followup study in 1983 which showed that operating procedures could be adjusted to meet the recommended standard for 100 percent quality improvement.

8. *Implementing actions.* This is the key step in suppliers' process control. Once an improved standard has been approved, a copy of the improved standard report is sent to the production manager for monitoring conformance to standards. The primary purpose of this monitoring is to make sure that valid information is circulated among the work force and necessary corrective action is taken.

9. *Analyzing goals.* Suppliers should consistently analyze and upgrade operational goals in terms of quality improvement. Pursuing quality improvement goes far beyond diagnosis and problem solving. It involves excellence in every task performed by every employee.

PURCHASING

Who is responsible for the quality of purchased products, buyers or suppliers? Usually suppliers are held responsible.[6] At Kawasaki purchasing managers are responsible for controlling the quality of purchased parts and for training suppliers to improve their quality. Training depends on the suppliers' quality and the type of relationship existing between buyer and supplier.

The least-developed relationship involves suppliers who ship out products uninspected as soon as they are manufactured. This means that the buyer's manufacturing division must engage in 100 percent inspection, which results in low product quality and high quality cost. Alternatively, some buyers inspect all materials and parts upon receipt, imposing a serious cost burden on the company and leaving no incentive for the supplier to become involved in a quality control program. One hundred percent inspection by both suppliers and buyers increases manufacturing costs. A more positive relationship develops when suppliers engage in 100 percent inspection in their manufacturing divisions. This gives the buyers the option of sampling inspection, but does not decrease the number of defective products requiring rework and does not decrease manufacturing costs. None of these alternatives is entirely satisfactory.

The ideal solution is for suppliers to establish a program that controls quality through the design, production, and shipping stages. This eliminates the need for receiving inspection, and results in rising quality level, lower manufacturing cost, and the establishment of a trusting relationship between buyers and suppliers.

However, properly organized QC programs do not always exist in supplier companies. To overcome this problem, it has become common practice for some companies to require their suppliers to use a fundamental form of QC program. Although using a basic program is better than no action, it falls far short of the goal of promoting the highest possible quality at the lowest price on a consistent basis.

Today, management studies from a wide array of sources show that it is virtually impossible for high quality to coexist with substandard suppliers. A long-term quality improvement program and the establishment of trusting relationships are necessary.

Logistics Quality Control

Designing and manufacturing high quality products is only part of the supplier's responsibility. Getting a quality product to buyers, with today's competition, is another major part. Therefore, to complete quality commitments, the QC program must extend to logistics, including distribution centers and consumer services.

DISTRIBUTION CENTERS

Suppliers often have the mistaken notion that quality control belongs to manufacturing operations and the application of QC programs stops at the manufacturing door. If this idea were correct, all the expense and effort put into meeting the buyer's requirements would become useless to the buyer if incorrect part numbers and quantities of goods, or damaged goods were shipped from distribution centers. Thus, suppliers' quality responsibility includes:

1. Checking the product before it is shipped to distribution centers, giving adequate quality assurance, and trying to find any deterioration in quality
2. Checking the percent defective at the time of delivery
3. Checking for wrong product sent, items misdirected, or orders not filled
4. Making sure the delivery date can be met at each step of distribution, aiming for on-time delivery
5. Checking the adequacy of packaging, transportation, and installation

Two courses of action are possible for a QC procedure: 100 percent inspection of product and orders to some predetermined quality level, or sampling inspection of products and orders. The first choice is clearly not acceptable—100-percent inspection is too time consuming and labor intensive. Alternatively, sampling determines some statistic common to the many different types and sizes of orders routinely shipped from manufacturing to distribution centers.

J. Martin, from Frame Autolite, described the procedure conducted randomly at that company. Shipment samples are selected from different categories such as small orders, large orders, or exports at the end of each shift. The selected samples are checked for nondefective items, right model, size, quantity, address, and time of delivery. If an error is found, the individual responsible must correct the error and transmit the relevant information to a data bank from which monthly reports are generated for the distribution manager.

The data is also used for direct comparison and statistical analysis at any level, including an individual shift or work center. In such cases the analysis can determine if a significant difference exists between two shifts or if the error rate is considerably higher in a particular work center. The final objective is to force the error percentage to zero by periodically lowering the number of errors.

The QC techniques used for direct comparison and controlling the error rate are regression, analysis of variance and control charts. The results obtained from these analyses are also added to the monthly data bank. However, it is extremely important that data generated by the system be analyzed for immediate corrective action to improve the quality of delivery.

CONSUMER SERVICES

The consumer, who is the final judge of products received from distribution centers, must be treated as a king or queen. Consumer demands may verge on the excessive, and bear little relation to the basic functions of the product; consumers may demand quality and features that are simply not economically feasible. But the efforts of suppliers to respond to these demands can have an enormous effect on quality perfection.

Quality control for consumer services has its own special requirements:

1. Controlling initial flow of new products, of new information, and feedback for product perfection
2. Determining the adequacy of instruction booklets and service manuals

3. Visiting the users and answering technological questions
4. Checking the ability of the system to perform immediate service or parts delivery
5. Checking the efficiency of periodic product inspection
6. Monitoring the degree of customer satisfaction
7. Detecting and/or predicting areas of basic consumer discontent
8. Collecting and analyzing information about defective or returned items
9. Utilizing customer information for product redesign and quality perfection

Managers, engineers, technicians, and QC personnel all play an important role in consumer service, not only in determining the supplier's success in meeting buyer's needs, but in maintaining high product safety standard.

To fulfill this obligation, QC must be integrated into all aspects of manufacturing. In our studies, we identified various types of QC techniques that have demonstrated their usefulness in suppliers' manufacturing operations. These techniques are classified with respect to their degree of importance for quality improvements and are briefly explained in the next section.

WHAT ARE THE ESSENTIAL QUALITY CONTROL TECHNIQUES?

Shewhart[3] defines quality control as the use of statistical techniques in manufacturing process. Deming[4] introduces a philosophy of statistical QC based on two fundamental ideas. First, the key to producing a consistent, high-quality product is control of the manufacturing process. Second, the key to successful process control is to distinguish between numerous small variations inherent in the process (common causes) and a few large structural variations (special causes). The causes of such variations can be disclosed through the application of QC techniques, which are classified as nonstatistical and statistical.

Nonstatistical Techniques

Two essential nonstatistical tools in disclosing the cause of quality variations are the cause-and-effect diagram (CED) and the checklist. The CED is a graphic analysis that displays the four factors (machinery, materials, manpower, and methods) affecting quality characteristics by sorting and relating them to the quality in a complex production process. The technique helps to pinpoint the causes of defects and allows a company to generate ways to improve quality. It also provides sufficient feedback to the previous stages to ensure that the origin of the problem is identified and corrected. By rectifying the problems and taking corrective action at every stage, continuous quality improvement results. A survey we conducted[5] has shown that 41 percent of respondents are using CED in manufacturing process control; 17 percent are using CED in design; 16 percent in R&D; 16 percent in logistics (see Table 10–2).

One of the companies that uses CED extensively for quality improvement is LTV Steel. LTV has provided an example of a task force that studied the problem of smudge spots on galvanized coils after annealing (see Figure 10–2). The CED identifies possible causes of the smudge spots in the four areas of machinery, manpower, materials, and methods. Once the causes were identified and verified, standards were changed to control the process and the smudge spots were eliminated.

Checklists are another nonstatistical tool that consists of a representative listing of factors (such as materials, component parts, or processes) that could affect quality. Suppliers can develop the necessary procedures to monitor and control each factor in the product development stages. Twenty-three percent of

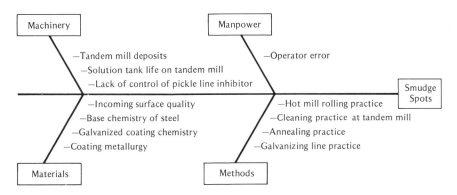

FIGURE 10–2   CED for Smudge Spot Problem

SOURCE: LTV Steel Company

TABLE 10–2. Percentage of QC Techniques Implemented in U.S. Firms

QC Techniques	Manufacturing Activities				
	Design	R&D	Manufacturing	Logistics	Not Used
NON-STATISTICAL					
Cause-and-effect Diagram	.17	.16	.41	.16	.33
Checklist	.23	.09	.53	.17	.18
STATISTICAL					
Fundamental methods					
100% inspection	.05	.01	.34	.16	.10
Sampling inspection	.03	.01	.92	.47	.02
Scatter diagram	.05	.02	.14	.05	.54
Pareto charts	.26	.20	.59	.19	.17
Frequency histogram	.29	.28	.69	.20	.07
X and Rm charts	.08	.06	.44	.13	.31
$\overline{X}$ and R charts	.13	.11	.76	.17	.13
$\overline{X}$ and s charts	.05	.04	.21	.06	.43
c charts	N/U	N/U	N/U	N/U	N/U
C charts	.03	.01	.26	.05	.50
u charts	N/U	N/U	N/U	N/U	N/U
U charts	.02	N/U	.15	.04	.47
P charts	.07	.06	.50	.11	.26
nP charts	.04	.02	.24	.02	.50
Process capability studies	N/U	N/U	.64	N/U	N/U
Advanced methods					
Correlation/ regression	.25	.27	.39	.13	.24
Analysis of variance	.24	.24	.23	.10	.24
Multivariate analysis	.08	.18	.15	.03	.50
Design of experiment	.30	.31	.30	.09	.28
Reliability techniques	.29	.21	.24	.10	.35
Operations research techniques	.08	.06	.09	.04	.50

N/U = Not used

firms use checklists in design, 9 percent in R&D, 50 percent in manufacturing process, and 17 percent in logistics.

Statistical Techniques

Statistical techniques deal with the collection, analysis, and interpretation of data related to causes of variation in quality characteristics. Statistical techniques can be categorized as either fundamental or advanced.[6]

FUNDAMENTAL STATISTICAL TECHNIQUES

Fundamental statistical techniques include sampling inspection, 100% inspection, scatter diagram, pareto histogram, frequency histogram, variable control charts, and attribute control charts. These are some of the techniques most widely used by U.S. buyers and suppliers.

Sampling Techniques Sampling techniques, including sampling inspection and 100% inspection, are used on finished products or parts to make after-the-fact decisions, such as whether to ship the product to the buyer or scrap it. These decisions are necessary when materials are received from a preceding subprocess or from a supplier.

Sampling looks at the quality of a part as an indication of the quality of the whole. This means that some bad parts will inevitably reach buyers. One hundred percent inspection calls for inspection of all products, and defectives are either repaired or discarded.

These two methods of inspection are not economically sound and will not improve supplier quality if they are the only methods of monitoring product quality, if inspection work is kept independent from operation work, and if the product is inspected after the production is completed.

Furthermore, these methods of QC impact buyers' quality to the extent that achieving quality excellence is impossible. Table 10–3 presents the impact of the supplier's QC method on the buyer's quality.

The lowest level of buyer's quality is when a supplier ships its uninspected products to buyers as soon as they are manufactured and the buyer, with no receiving inspection, sends them directly to the manufacturing operation, thus engaging manufac-

TABLE 10–3. Impact of Supplier's QC on Buyer's Quality

SUPPLIERS			BUYERS		
Design Control	Manufacturing Control	Logistics Control	Receiving Inspection	Manufacturing Control	Final Quality Level
N/U	N/U	N/U		100% inspection	Poor
N/U	N/U	N/U	100% inspection	Sampling	Low
N/U	N/U	100% inspection	100% inspection	N/U	Moderate
N/U	100% inspection	100% inspection	Sampling inspection	N/U	Satisfactory
N/U	Process control	Sampling	N/U	N/U	High
Design control	Process control	Sampling	N/U	N/U	Excellent

N/U = No QC used

turing in 100% inspection which results in high scrap and rework and poor finished goods quality.

Alternatively, some buyers inspect all materials and parts upon receipt and conduct sample inspections in manufacturing. Not only does this method not improve quality, it imposes a serious cost burden on the buyer and leaves no incentive for the supplier to become involved in QC.

One hundred percent inspection by the supplier and buyer in manufacturing, logistics, and receiving areas results in moderate or satisfactory final quality, but increases manufacturing costs through the dual cost of inspection and higher rejection. Engaging suppliers in manufacturing process control and integrating sampling with their logistics activities significantly improves the cost and quality of final goods.

In the ideal situation, the supplier's design division (with the cooperation of the buyer's designers) controls quality at the design level, manufacturing process, and logistics. In such an instance, the buyer's inspection will be reduced drastically or completely eliminated at the receiving point. This reduction will be accompanied by achievement of excellent quality and establishment of reliable quality relation between buyers and suppliers.

Thus, supplier quality improvement starts with logical analysis of process data to arrive at a decision on process control. Techniques include the scatter diagram, pareto histogram, frequency histogram, and control charts.

Scatter Diagram Improving quality necessitates determining if the manufacturing process is stable (in statistical control). The presence of pattern, trend or cycle indicates that the process is not stable and causes should be identified as well as pattern and trend. A scatter diagram is used to find the extent of the relationship between one cause and another cause or the relationship between two factors affecting product quality. Only 14 percent of the respondents apply the scatter diagram in process control; even fewer use it for other activities.

The Pareto Histogram The pareto histogram assumes that a few problems are always significant in severity or frequency of occurrence. In either case, these problems are costly. The histogram determines the relative frequency of various problems or causes for problems so that primary attention can be focused on the most important ones to reduce cost and improve productivity. The pareto histogram is used by 59 percent of firms in the manufacturing process, 26 percent for design, 20 percent for R&D, 19 percent in logistics.

The Frequency Histogram This technique is a process of arranging information derived from product characteristics in numerical order and frequency. It aids quality improvement by revealing information about the normality of the distribution, central tendency, and standard deviation.

Any process will contain a multitude of variables, such as raw materials, operations, machines, and so on that may be the source of two variables: common causes and special causes. If only common causes of variation are present, the output of a process forms the systematic pattern of a normal distribution. But if special causes of variation are present, the process output is not stable over time and its pattern is not predictable. The frequency histogram can be used to identify the presence of special causes of variation.

A frequency histogram also reveals central tendency, which describes the value of a distribution that is expected to occur most often, and standard deviation, the degree to which numerical information tends to spread about the central value.

The frequency histogram is used by 69 percent of the firms for manufacturing process, 29 percent for design, 28 percent for R&D, and 20 percent in logistics.

Although frequency and pareto histograms help in product and process analysis, their use is limited because they do not separate the causes of variations. Control charts are the most powerful tools to detect the causes of variation.

Control Charts Control charts are time-based graphic comparisons of actual product-quality characteristics with predetermined limits (defined by design engineers) for the product. An important distinction in the technical use of these charts is between variable control charts and attribute control charts.

Variable control charts include X and Rm charts, $\overline{X}$ and R charts, and $\overline{X}$ and s charts. These techniques identify an actual measured quality characteristic, such as dimension, and indicate if the process is controlled and the product is consistent.

X and Rm charts (for controlling one item per sample) are used by 44 percent of firms for process control and by 13 percent for logistics. $\overline{X}$ and R charts (for controlling 2 to 7 parts per sample) are used by 76 percent of the manufacturers for process control, 13 percent in design, 13 percent in R&D, and 17 percent in logistics.

$\overline{X}$ and s charts are used when there are more than seven parts per sample. Only 21 percent of the firms surveyed use this technique for process control. All of these variable control charts are applied by considerably fewer firms in other manufacturing activities.

Attribute control charts identify characteristics for products that should be visually inspected for defects, such as cracks or missing components. Attribute charts are divided into defects and defectives, with two subclassifications of equal sample size and unequal sample size.

Attribute charts with equal sample size are called c charts for one defect per sample, and C charts for multiple defects per sample. Our analysis of the questionnaires indicated that none of the firms surveyed are using c charts, and only 26 percent are using C charts for process control. Significantly fewer firms have implemented C charts in other areas.

Attribute charts for controlling the number of defects for unequal sample size are u charts for one defect per unit, and U charts for multiple defects per unit. No respondents use u charts, and only 15 percent of the respondents are using U charts for process control.

Attribute charts to control defectives are P charts for equal sample size, and nP charts for unequal sample size. P and nP charts are used by 50 percent and 24 percent of the firms, respectively, for process control with considerably fewer manufacturers using them in other activities.

These charts are used to determine if the products in question are within specifications, but they cannot determine if the process is capable of producing products satisfactorily.

Process Capability Studies Process capability studies provide an indication of process and quality improvement as a company seeks greater uniformity around design specifications. In practice, the important effects are improving the value of the ratio for process capability and thus the reliability of products. This technique is used by 64 percent of respondents for manufacturing process.

ADVANCED SQC METHODS

Advanced statistical methods, such as correlation/regression, analysis of variance, experimental design, multivariate analysis, various methods of operations research, and reliability engineering techniques, are used by engineers and industrial statisticians for solving complicated problems. An example would be selection of the optimum level of factors that influence quality of product. These techniques help to analyze the interaction of factors in design and R&D and help to reduce the variability inherent in the manufacturing process where workers have minimal need for control charts or inspections.

Correlation/regression is used by 39 percent of firms for process control and 27 percent and 25 percent for R&D and design engineering. Analysis of variance is used by 23 percent for process control and 24 percent for R&D and design. These two methods are also used by a few companies for other activities.

Techniques of engineering reliability are implemented by 24 percent of surveyed companies for process control, 29 percent for design, and 21 percent for R&D. Multivariate analysis and experimental design are used by 15 percent and 30 percent respectively. These two methods are used by 8 percent and 30 percent for design and 18 percent and 31 percent for R&D.

Techniques of operations research are used by 9 percent, 8 percent, and 6 percent of respondents for process control, design, and R&D. Few firms use advanced methods of quality control in other manufacturing activities.

WHY ARE SOME FIRMS SLOW TO IMPLEMENT QC TECHNIQUES?

Our study revealed that the implementation of QC techniques has been slow in U.S. firms. In some cases, the companies studied were not even familiar with such fundamental and constructive quality control techniques as CED (33 percent) or scatter diagram (54 percent). Reasons contributing to the slow implementation of QC techniques in some areas are presented in Table 10–4. The problems considered most serious are lack of employee mathematical skills and lack of top management participation in QC programs.

Only about 5 percent of the companies, for example, reported no serious problem with their employees' math skills. The remaining 95 percent indicated some type of problem in this area. Also, only 14 percent of the companies responding indicated no problem in gaining the full participation of top management; 86 percent indicated they did not have full support of top management in QC programs.

Other problems associated with the slow QC implementation are lack of supervisor's support, lack of communication within the company on QC, lack of support from design engineers, lack of supplier/buyer support, lack of production personnel support, and finally, high cost of QC implementation.

Even with these problems, however, the quality improvement and benefits gained have been so impressive that the situation stimulates greater interest among suppliers and buyers for

TABLE 10–4. Reasons for Slow Implementation of QC Techniques

	Estimated Degree of Problems			
Problems	None 1	Some 2	Much 3	Very much 4
Lack of employee mathematical skill	5%	41%	33%	21%
Lack of top management participation in QC programs	14	32	26	28
Lack of supervisor support	14	42	32	12
Lack of communication within the company on QC	14	51	24	11
Lack of support from design engineering	21	49	20	10
Lack of suppliers support	21	49	23	7
Lack of production worker support	24	55	14	7
Lack of top management support	34	42	14	10
High cost of implementation	38	46	10	6

further QC implementation rather than counteracting their involvement.

WHAT BENEFITS CAN BE OBTAINED FROM QUALITY CONTROL PROGRAMS?

QC programs have proved to be a competitive weapon for many years for the Japanese. They have infused quality control techniques into all aspects of a product's life with a philosophy that is integrated throughout the entire organizational structure. Today, this weapon has been discovered by a few American suppliers and the techniques have been implemented in three areas; product design, manufacturing process, and logistics (including distribution and consumer services).

Product Design Benefits

The significant improvements experienced from the implementation of QC during the design phase, reported by the American Supplier Institute, are summarized here.[2]

1. Product performance variability inherent in design is reduced by identification of the major control factors for manufacturing.
2. Individual product components are optimized so that variation due to uncontrolled factors has a minimum impact on product performance.
3. Ways can be found to slow the rate of deterioration after the product is used for a period of time.
4. Weeks of testing can be reduced to minutes spent analyzing many variables and the interactions among them.
5. Process variability is reduced and optimum conditions for manufacturing reliable products can be defined.
6. Costs of raw materials and experimentations are reduced.
7. Substantial savings are possible due to extended tool life and reduced downtime.
8. Product quality and plant efficiency are improved.

Manufacturing Process Benefits

The benefits gained from the use of QC techniques extends to the manufacturing process. Production workers using QC during operations can pinpoint causes of defects and either eliminate these causes or pass the information to design engineers. The problems related to process or design can be prevented at the source, thereby leading to enhancement of quality. The tangible advantages for suppliers are producing high-quality products, improving process capability, and reducing scrap, rework, returned items, and inspection time for work in process and finished goods inventory. The intangible benefits are improvement of workers' morale and buyers' satisfaction.

SQC implementation in the manufacturing process has contributed to some excellent short-term results. For example, Motorola reported the following improvements in 1984:

1. Scrap was reduced 53 percent, resulting in annualized savings of more than $400,000.

2. Repair costs were cut by more than 10 percent.
3. Throughput composite yield improved by more than 50 percent, with each individual yield point averaging over 9 percent.
4. Outstanding final quality performance of thick film ignition (TFI).
5. Silicon captive absolute pressure sensor (SCAPS) final quality defects decreased more than 85 percent by December 1984.
6. Customer warranty returns improved more than 70 percent for SCAPS and 30 percent for TFI.
7. On-time delivery reached 100 percent and stayed there consistently.

In general, productivity at Motorola improved significantly. For some operations, the quality improved *200 percent.*

One-year QC implementation for manufacturing techniques at Goodyear resulted in dramatically reduced manufacturing tolerance of the poly-V belt. Tolerance for the belts had been ±3.2 millimeters (mm) to 7.2 mm center-to-center, depending on belt length. Goodyear's new manufacturing process is capable of producing to a tolerance of ±2 mm. to 2–5 mm. center-to-center for different length poly-V belts. Significant improvement in productivity has resulted.

Implementation of QC at Boeing has been expanded from one pilot project in January 1985 to fifteen ongoing projects and has resulted in more than a 75 percent reduction in errors in graphics and a 50 percent reduction in variability of paint thickness in one division.

The Hewlett-Packard quality improvement program initiated in 1985 led to a 5 percent reduction per year in failure rate for small products and a 65 percent reduction per year for large products. Quality improved about 25 percent and units per hour per person increased by 10 percent. Utilizing a quality improvement program in a molding operation saved $2000 per month. Product goals for 1985 were established at 99 percent for first-time yields. The first-time rate was 85 to 90 percent, with 50 to 70 percent reduction in scrap and rework. The external failure rate improved tenfold. Through this quality and productivity improvement, Hewlett-Packard captured a large market share in 1985.

Evaluating production improvements in Matsushita Electric Industrial Company revealed a reduction in warranty costs by a 9 to 1 ratio, a rework rate under 2 percent, and an external failure rate of less than 1 percent. The defect rate decreased from 3.2 percent to 1.7 percent, and the claim-to-sales ratio was reduced by 5.6 percent from January 1983 to December 1985.

Logistics Benefits

One of the greatest benefits of QC implementation comes from its use in distribution centers and consumer services. The application of QC techniques in distribution centers will drastically reduce the costs incurred by shipment of defective items, incorrect models, incorrect sizes or quantities, incorrect addresses, and most importantly, early or late delivery. The use of QC for logistics also assures improvements in supplier-buyer relationships, consumers' goodwill, and the company's reputation.

QC for consumer services benefits the suppliers' manufacturing system in all aspects of product quality that affect the buyers' point of view, such as:

1. Controlling initial flow of new product, of new information, and feedback for product perfection
2. Determining the adequacy of instruction booklets and service manuals
3. Visiting the users and answering technological questions
4. Checking the ability of the system to perform immediate service or parts delivery
5. Checking the efficiency of periodic product inspection
6. Monitoring the degree of customer satisfaction
7. Detecting and/or predicting areas of basic consumer discontent
8. Collecting and analyzing information about defective/returned items
9. Utilizing customer information for product redesign and quality perfection

Regardless of the advantages obtained from the implementation of QC methods in product design, manufacturing process, and logistics, the practitioners, including managers, engineers, technicians, operation personnel, and QC personnel, play an important role in determining the suppliers' success in meeting buyers' needs and in achieving quality excellence. Their contribution in assuring the required quality, reliability, and safety of the buyers' products make them responsible and highly respected members of society.

SUMMARY

A survey of current QC practices among U.S. manufacturers (buyers and suppliers) suggests some tentative conclusions. First, implementation of QC in suppliers' systems consistently improves product quality through quality control during design, the manufacturing process, and logistics. From a quality point of view, the use of advanced and fundamental QC techniques and S/N in engineering design ratio offers many potential advantages to suppliers. This approach calls for designing products and process that are robust against both external and internal factors by removing the effect of causes instead of removing the causes themselves. Consequently, products are manufactured more uniformly and perform more consistently in service under a variety of conditions.

Second, implementation of QC in the manufacturing process improves product quality by reducing errors and decreasing scrap, rework, and returned items. QC provides knowledge for diagnosing problems, removing the causes, and improving process to produce according to design specifications.

A QC program in logistics (distribution centers and consumer services) is the most promising area of contribution to quality improvement. QC techniques help to prevent the shipment of defective items and incorrect models or quantity to buyers. The techniques are also helpful in direct comparisons of different manufacturing shifts, centers, or divisions to determine the high error areas and correct them.

The use of QC programs for consumer services helps to control the initial flow of products and information and provide feedback for design engineers, manufacturing production, and logistics. This information is not only used for quality perfection but also for increasing customers' satisfaction.

Most suppliers are in the preliminary stages of QC implementation. QC techniques have been used extensively in manufacturing process, but the majority of surveyed firms did not use QC techniques in design and engineering, research and development, and logistics. The main reasons for this seem to be lack of employee basic math skills and lack of top management participation in QC programs. Because of this limited implementation, U.S. firms have not really tested the full effect of QC on quality improvement. One positive way for Americans to meet foreign challenges and to produce consistently high product quality is for U.S suppliers to seriously consider adopting QC techniques in all manufacturing areas.

The benefits obtained from QC implementation by a number of companies have been very impressive in terms of quality. Such a continuous application has as its target quality excellence.

CHAPTER 11

What Is the Impact of QC Techniques and JIT on Quality Cost?

QC techniques and JIT provide a favorable environment for reducing quality cost.

IN THE PREVIOUS CHAPTER we described a permanent quality program that attains a superior position in the marketplace by producing world-class quality in every production line. High quality output alone, however, is not enough. The cost of achieving that quality must be managed carefully so that long-range costs do not impact negatively on an organization's productivity.[1]

Many experts in operations management and manufacturing disciplines believe that the key to an organization's productivity is its quality system. The forces that shape this system are QC programs and just-in-time production.[2,3] Therefore, this chapter addresses the issue of how QC and JIT reduce quality cost. First, the concept of a quality cost system is discussed to explain the relationships among JIT, QC, and manufacturing cost. Then, the impact of QC techniques on quality cost is described. Next, models for making three quality decisions, including quality of design, quality of conformance, and quality of delivery are discussed. The idea is to distinguish among three choices to illustrate the basic trade-offs between cost and quality. Finally, the impact of JIT production on quality cost is discussed.

WHAT IS THE CONCEPT OF QUALITY COST?

The concept of the quality cost system can be traced to the 1950s when it was introduced to highlight the cost of poor performance—the cost of not making a product right the first time. J. Juran defines quality cost as the ratio to sales of any manufacturing costs in excess of what would have been incurred if the product had been built right the first time. Quality is measured by the degree of conformation to an established level; cost is associated with the lack of conformation in four dimensions: (1) internal failure cost, (2) external failure cost, (3) prevention cost, and (4) appraisal cost.[4]

The four-dimension quality cost presented in Table 11–1 can arise for two reasons. First, the possibility exists that the manufactured product does not conform to design specifications. Second, the possibility exists that the manufactured product *might not* conform to design specifications.[5]

Product Does Not Conform
to Specification

The first type of quality cost arises because the manufactured product does not conform to design specifications, and is classified as internal failure cost or external failure cost.

Internal failure cost is the cost of product failures discovered in-house prior to installation or shipment to the customer. It includes all rework and scrap resulting from the lack of capability to produce 100-percent conforming products. It also includes the costs associated with failure analysis used to determine the cause of product failure; reinspection of products that have been reworked; and downgrading, which is the price differential be-

TABLE 11–1. The Four-Dimension Quality Cost

Product Does not Conform to Specification	Product Might not Conform to Specification
Internal Failure Cost	*Prevention Cost*
a. Scrap	a. Quality and reliability administration
b. Rework	
c. Failure analysis	b. A strategic quality program
d. Reinspection	c. Training of personnel
e. Downgrading	d. Preventive maintenance of equipment
	e. Standardization of equipment
External Failure Cost	*Appraisal Cost*
a. Rejected and returned items	a. Incoming inspection
b. Repair	b. In-process and final inspection
c. Warranty	c. Production and inspection equipment
d. Installation failure	
e. Incorrect delivery	e. Quality and reliability audits
	f. Vendor rating

tween normal selling price and reduced price of reworked products.

External failure cost is composed of the cost of product deficiencies discovered during installation or after delivery to the customer. It consists of repair cost of returned items, warranty cost, installation failure cost, and the cost of replacement associated with incorrect delivery.

From a supplier viewpoint, there is a major difference between failure discovered in-house and that discovered by the customer. Internal failure cost is what Feigenbaum refers to as the hidden plant—an unexpected opportunity for productivity improvement. But external failures are individually more critical, affecting both cost and reputation.

External failure cost comprises more than it might seem to at first; it includes buyers who refuse to buy a product because of problems they have had in the past. It also includes buyers who turn away from a product because of bad publicity about a supplier. Furthermore, intangible losses can arise because of a decline in workers' morale, production delays, and an insufficient overhead recovery.

Product Might Not Conform
to Specification

The second type of quality cost, which arises because the manufactured product might not conform to design specifications, can be subdivided into prevention cost or appraisal cost.

Prevention cost represents deliberate investment by a firm in order to avoid manufacturing defective parts. It is the basis of quality and incorporates the following: quality and reliability administration, a strategic quality program, training of engineers, inspectors, and production personnel, preventive maintenance of equipment, and standardization of equipment.

Appraisal cost represents an investment that may be made freely by a company or may be imposed upon it by a major buyer. The cost is associated with monitoring the existing quality of products and with identifying faulty products before they are completed or delivered to the buyer. Appraisal cost items include incoming inspection, vendor rating, in-process and final inspection of products, production and inspection equipment, and quality and reliability audits.

Of the four dimensions of quality cost, those caused by external failure are deemed the most costly. When defective parts are not corrected from their sources, there is a dramatic reduction in productivity and an escalation in quality cost. Richard Anderson, general manager of the computer system division of Hewlett-Packard, supports this viewpoint by describing the damage caused by a faulty 2-cent resistor. If workers catch the resistor before it is used, the company loses 2 cents. If they find it after it has been soldered into a computer component, it costs the company about $10 to repair the part. If they do not find the resistor until it is in the customer's hands, the repair could cost hundreds of dollars. Indeed, if a $5,000 computer has to be repaired in the field, expenses may exceed the original manufacturing cost.[6]

Quality cost at the beginning of the 1970s was 10 percent of the sales dollars in numerous U.S. manufacturing organizations. The cost level reached 20 percent in 1980 and was expected to increase again unless manufacturers took action to control cost.[7]

Action to control overall quality cost starts with placing more emphasis on the reduction of quality cost on the factory floor. Low quality cost requires a high quality of design, which is the responsibility of design engineers. It also depends on the supplier's material, the ability of production workers and quality control personnel to build products to specification, and the quality of products delivered to buyers—the responsibility of distribution centers and customer services.

Relying on the ability of personnel at every stage from design to delivery necessitates systematic measurement to assess their performance. A quality cost system measures personnel performance in two ways: it allows identification of the investment made to prevent nonconformities and errors, and it reveals loopholes and problems that prevent a company from attaining the necessary performance.

HOW CAN QC TECHNIQUES REDUCE QUALITY COST?

A survey was conducted in 1983 to determine the actual distribution of quality cost in 35 American manufacturing firms. One would hope to see a distribution of quality cost expenditures on prevention and appraisal activities skewed to over 50 percent. Only 25 percent of the companies, however, reported spending more than 50 percent of total quality cost on prevention, and only 38 percent reported spending more than 50 percent on appraisal. Internal and external failure cost exceeded 50 percent of total quality cost in nearly one-fourth of the companies that responded.[8]

Thus, if this data can be generalized, it is obvious that an effective approach is needed to reduce external cost. A firm could decrease both internal and external failure cost by increasing investment in prevention and appraisal costs. Increasing appraisal costs can identify defective units before they are shipped to customers. However, this approach, which dominates quality control policies in many U.S. plants, is likely to result in additional internal failure cost since the identified defects must be reworked or scrapped. It is thus questionable whether total cost can be reduced by investing in appraisal cost.

Improving manufacturing productivity depends on improving quality cost. The total quality cost in any firm should not be more than 4 percent of sales, with the largest part (2.5 percent) devoted to prevention and appraisal costs. One percent of sales should be for internal failure cost, and external failure cost should not exceed 0.5 percent of the sales dollar.[9] The Japanese automobile industry lends credibility to this suggestion by showing total quality cost in the 2.5 to 4 percent range. This is in sharp contrast to the 25 percent quality cost in the U.S. auto industry.[10]

A new approach, which is widely used among Japanese manufacturers, is to concentrate efforts and dollars on the prevention of nonconformities, since the cost of preventing defective units is less than the cost of identifying and fixing defects. This approach emphasizes the use of models for quality decision problems. The goal of developing the models is to analyze the relationship between quality and quality cost and find an optimal point for quality at which the total costs are minimal.

WHAT ARE SOME MODELS FOR MAKING QUALITY DECISIONS?

The objective of any manufacturing firm is to bring total quality cost to a minimum while maintaining or improving product quality. The following quality design, quality conformance, and quality delivery decision models are presented to illustrate the trade-offs between quality and quality cost.

Quality of Design

Most buyers would agree that quality assessment is based on the relative expected value of the services provided by the products. The high quality of a product, however, refers to its quality of design subject to quality-cost considerations.

Design engineers enhance the quality of design in three major phases:

1. System design—the design of and experimentation with materials, parts, components, and the assembly system
2. Parameter design—the choice of the best combination of materials or parts that diminish the effect of outer conditions (e.g., humidity or temperature) and inner conditions (e.g., deterioration of product) while keeping product performance as strong as possible
3. Tolerance design—the determination of how much variation from the target specification can be allowed by taking

ing into consideration both the loss due to deviating
from parameter design and the cost of different grades of
components.[11]

Design and experimentation account for large expenditures
in quality cost because design engineers must achieve several design objectives while developing a product that may have several
hundred elements. Appraisal and prevention costs are assumed
zero at zero conformance. The costs become infinitely larger as
the defect rate approaches zero. There is, however, an optimum
quality of design that presents a unique quality conformance with
feasible quality cost. Above the optimal point, the increasing appraisal and prevention costs for achieving greater quality of design more than offset the greater value of the finished products.
Below the optimum, the reduction in appraisal and prevention
costs results in a greater reduction in the quality of products.

Quality of Conformance

This model relates to the fidelity with which the product conforms to the design specification. A well-manufactured product
and a poorly manufactured product may have the same quality of
design, but they differ in quality of conformance. If no quality
control organization exists, prevention costs are usually very low
and failure and appraisal costs are correspondingly high. Typical
ratios in the absence of a quality control system are: failure cost,
70 percent; appraisal cost, 25 percent; and prevention cost, 5 percent of total quality cost. The sum of these costs frequently accounts for about 20 to 25 percent or more of the total cost of
production.[12]

Although the ratio varies from one type of production process to another, it should be possible to reduce the total quality
cost in many cases. The quality of conformance decision model
suggests that a small increase in prevention cost can reduce failures and appraisal cost by a greater amount, thus reducing the
total cost. This trend will continue until all the obvious remedies
have been made. The optimum quality level is discovered by finding the point at which prevention cost starts to rise by a greater
amount than the corresponding savings in failure and appraisal
cost.

Based on this suggestion and other clear evidence (such as
Japanese quality success as a result of defect prevention pro-

grams), it is obvious that investment in both prevention and appraisal are necessary to reduce product defects and decrease total quality cost. But investing exclusively in appraisal may lead to unacceptable cost. The protection that appraisal programs afford the company's reputation is a fragile shield that will crumble, taking a large share of productivity with it.

In quality of design and quality of conformance models, the issue of loss of customer satisfaction due to a defective product or incorrect delivery is avoided. Customer dissatisfaction may eventually destroy a company's reputation in the marketplace. Thus, we suggest manufacturers implement the *quality of delivery* decision model.

Quality of Delivery

This model depicts the relationship between the percent of incorrect or defective items and the degree of customer satisfaction corresponding to total quality costs. According to this model, as presented in Figure 11–1, if distribution centers ship their products without any inspection the cost of appraisal is negligible, but the higher percentage of defective or incorrect deliveries leads to low customer satisfaction. Engaging distribution centers in quality control increases appraisal cost and decreases the percentage of defective parts or incorrect delivery. This improvement leads

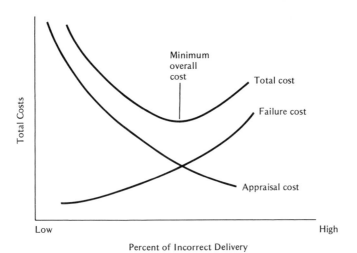

FIGURE 11–1   Optimal Level of Quality of Delivery

to higher customer satisfaction and enhances a firm's reputation. The improvement, however, must be analyzed as to its impact on total costs, because above the optimum quality delivery point more investment in quality delivery jeopardizes the organization's productivity.

Based on these three models, practitioners must realize two things. First, implementation of QC techniques in suppliers' companies can affect the rate of cost decline in three ways:

1. Reduction in time for design and experimentation and substitution of the least expensive materials for better quality
2. Optimization of manufacturing process
3. Reduction of quality cost including internal failure cost and external failure cost

Second, productivity and quality management must be viewed simultaneously. Otherwise quality improvement programs that appear to be successful may result in a negative impact on the organization's productivity. Thus quality improvement depends upon balancing costs of the quality programs and obtained quality.

HOW CAN JIT REDUCE QUALITY COST?

Further improvement in quality cost can be obtained by the practice of JIT in manufacturing systems. The JIT system is considered a major factor in contributing to the success of Japanese companies that achieve high quality with low manufacturing cost. This can be seen clearly when U.S. and Japanese auto companies are compared. According to one estimate, the JIT system gives Japanese industries a $500 per car advantage in cost.

The primary objective of the JIT technique is the improvement of quality through the elimination of waste. From 15 to 40 percent of the quality cost for almost any American product is for embedded waste.[13] Waste in manufacturing is classified as inventory, the production of defective items, and the related costs.

JIT demands that inventory be kept to a minimum. Extra supply adds extra cost of quality and forces an operation to tie up capital that could be invested elsewhere. A significant reduction in producing defective items can be achieved by the elimination of inventory. Defective parts can be detected promptly and fast feedback given to the design and production process, allowing prompt identification and correction of the problems. This reduction decreases the amount of inspection and resource commitment necessary for confirming non-defective products, thus resulting in more cost savings.

In addition to reduction of defective items, elimination of inventory results in a significant reduction in cost of transportation, materials handling, and delay time involved between production processes. With zero inventory, there is no need for a profusion of warehouses, fleets of forklift trucks, tons of racks, hundreds of employees to move the inventory, weeks or sometimes months of waiting for goods to be processed, and millions of dollars to maintain materials.

The implementation of JIT production necessitates changes in other phases of manufacturing in a plant, such as small lot sizes, set-up time reduction, uniform scheduling, group technology, and kanban systems. Each of these changes can result in a further reduction in manufacturing cost.

Small Lot Size

With minimum inventory in the system, any fluctuation in production at the final assembly line (such as unsatisfactory product) would create variations in production requirements in preceding stages. The variation becomes larger for the processes farther away from the final assembly line. To prevent variance in production requirements, production should be held at its minimum quantity size, ideally a lot size of one. Small lot sizes help to reduce nonconformities through the quick detection and solution of problems, through accurate and simplified data collection for process analysis and quality analysis, and through elimination of losses due to large contracts. For example, Commodore International had a contract with the Japanese for 170,000 disk drives for a special model of personal computer. The whole shipment was rejected due to nonconforming product. With a small lot size, such a loss could be prevented by suspending production and eliminating the problem.[14]

Set-Up Time Reduction

A major obstacle in producing small lots is set-up time. Long set-up time makes the small lot production uneconomical. By cutting the set-up time, machine downtime and work in process are reduced, and so are the costs associated with obsolescence, materials handling, materials control, and quality control.

In addition to these cost reductions, short set-up time leads to shorter lead time (total time required to manufacture an item). As a result of short lead time and small inventory, manufacturers will have much more flexibility for adapting to changes in the market or changes due to other factors.

Uniform Scheduling

Short set-up time permits uniform scheduling throughout a production facility. This is a planning method for smooth production flow that requires the consumption of critical resources in the same increments or time duration at each opportunity. This requirement leads to reduced daily scheduling, reduced inventory, and material handling.

Utilizing Group Technology

Machines with different functions can be grouped according to the required production steps of one or a family of items. With this approach, functions that were performed in separate work stations can be performed in one place. Workers are then trained to handle different jobs in one work station. Utilizing a group technology (GT) approach can result in significant cost reduction and manufacturing flexibility due to reduction of lead time, which in turn results from reductions in throughput time, set-up time, and elimination of non-value added process time (such as inspection).

Further cost reductions are related to reduction of work in process and finished goods inventories, reduction of total labor costs, simplified process plans, quality control by operations personnel, reduced materials handling, utilization of resources, materials management, and quality control.

Other areas of potential cost reduction are engineering design and process planning. In the engineering phase, the design for a new part initially requires an investigation into whether a similar part has been designed. Given the high turnover in technical personnel, design proliferation becomes a way of life. Thus, identifying critical attributes for each part type, coding them, and sorting them in a data base facilitates subsequent retrieval of this data. If jointly used with computer aided design, engineering lead time can be reduced drastically. This can also lead to more reliable design and higher quality products.

With respect to process planning, GT reduces the preparation time of new routings from hours to minutes. It also greatly improves process plans owing to standardized operation terminology. Factory floor space is utilized more efficiently, usually by a factor of two or more, and the number of forklifts required is significantly reduced. Furthermore, such changes shorten the lead time by a factor of at least one.

Pull System

This execution system activates production and consumption events using kanban. Pull systems demand reduction of inventory at every step of production. This requires discipline, self-regulation, and linked processes with an accurate and fast system of communication. All of these requirements lead to reduced manufacturing costs due to reduction in inventory and material handling, shorter lead time, and decreased administrative efforts.

WHAT IS THE COMBINED IMPACT OF JIT AND QC ON QUALITY COST?

The JIT system seems to be the ultimate way of organizing the production of standard products. But the system is premised on consistently high quality. Industries using JIT cannot function with a conventional approach to quality—the inspect-and-fix mode. The preferred approach is the standardization of product through QC, which signals poor quality as it occurs and reduces the possibility of making scrap.

The Japanese moved strongly into a JIT manufacturing system because they relied heavily on QC programs. They made a great deal of effort to solve quality problems first. This requires substantial time and commitment to training, problem solving, and establishing continuous quality improvement.

JIT should be adopted in two sequential stages, with quality problems solved first, then quantity. Both JIT and QC demand simplicity and high quality in manufacturing processes. JIT simplifies the manufacturing process by employing the kanban system. QC simplifies the manufacturing process by reducing the variability of process output, not just meeting specifications.

The tight inventory requirement of the JIT system offers a further quality and cost-improvement opportunity. The system will not work if nonconforming products are produced frequently. There is an inescapable pressure for both exposing and solving problems. This pressure may be considered an opportunity to make improvements. QC exposes the patterns and location of problems in processes and provides the tools to eliminate the problems. As soon as the causes of the exposed problems are eliminated, more and more inventory can be pulled from the system, which forces other problems to the surface. The ultimate result is better quality with lower manufacturing costs.

SUMMARY

High product quality at lower cost is the result of a better manufacturing control system—namely JIT production and QC techniques. Implementation of QC techniques reduces quality cost through a reduction in time for design, substitution of less expensive material, a decrease in experimentation and testing, a reduction in the manufacturing process, a reduction in process control and product inspection, and reduction of failure costs.

JIT reduces quality cost through reduction in producing defective items, elimination of inventory, and utilization of manufacturing resources. JIT and QC programs are not one-time efforts that can easily and quickly be implemented. Rather they are systems that require continuous application and assessment to achieve a sustained improvement in quality. They also require the continuous close cooperation and communication of management with personnel at all levels of industry.

Notes

Chapter 1. Why Have Japan's Product Quality and Productivity Increased?

1. C. Y. Yang. "Management Styles: American Vis-à-Vis Japanese." *Columbia Journal of World Business,* Vol. 12, No. 3, Fall 1977, pp. 23–31.
2. A. Lizuka. "Japanese Business leaders: How Do They Rise to the Top?" *The Wheel Extended,* Vol. 11, No. 4, October–December 1981, pp. 9–15.
3. B. B. Tregoe. "Productivity in America: Where It Went and How to Get It Back." *Management Review,* Vol. 72, No. 2, February 1983, pp. 23–45.
4. H. Takeuchi. "Productivity: Learning from the Japanese." *California Management Review,* Vol. 23, No. 4, Summer 1981, pp. 5–19.
5. R. T. Johnson and W. G. Ouchi. "Made In America (Under Japanese Management)." *Harvard Business Review,* September–October 1974, pp. 61–69.
6. T. Hain. "Japanese Management in the United States." In S. M. Lee and G. Schwendiman. *Management by Japanese Systems.* New York: Praeger Publishers, 1982.
7. W. Ouchi. *Theory Z: How American Business Can Meet the Japanese Challenge.* Reading, Mass.: Addison-Wesley Publishing Company, 1981.
8. Y. Tsurumi. "Productivity: The Japanese Approach." *Pacific Basin Quarterly,* No. 6, Summer 1981, pp. 7–9.
9. K. Sakakibara. "Creativity Development in Japanese Industry." *The Wheel Extended,* Vol. 2, No. 2, Autumn 1972, pp. 13–18.
10. R. W. Hall. *Driving the Productivity Machine: Production Planning and Control in Japan.* Falls Church, Va.: American Production and Inventory Control Society, Inc., Fall 1981.
11. R. H. Hayes and W. J. Abernathy. "Managing Our Way to Economic Decline." *Harvard Business Review,* July-August 1980, pp. 67–77.
12. J. C. Abegglen. *Management and Worker.* Tokyo: Sophia University Tokyo, 1973.
13. E. F. Vogel. *Japan As Number One: Lessons for America,* Cambridge, Mass.: Harvard University Press, 1979.

153

14. I. Tamura. "Part 2: Sharp Contrast Between Booming and Depressed Sectors Marked Industry." *Industrial Review of Japan*, 1982, pp. 41–42.
15. R. H. Hayes. "Why Japanese Factories Work." *Harvard Business Review*, July-August 1981, pp. 57–66.
16. A. M. Whitehill and S. Takezawa. "Workplace Harmony: Another Japanese 'Miracle'?" *Columbia Journal of World Business*, Vol. 13, No. 3, Fall 1978, pp. 25–39.
17. R. J. Schonberger. *Japanese Manufacturing Techniques: Nine Hidden Lessons in Simplicity*. New York: The Free Press, 1982.
18. R. B. Reich. *The Next American Frontiers*. New York: Times Books, 1983.
19. S. C. Wheelwright. "Japan—Where Operations Really Are Strategic." *Harvard Business Review*, July-August 1981, pp. 67–74.
20. J. M. Juran. "Product Quality—A Prescription for the West: Part I: Training and Improvement Programs." *Management Review*, Vol. 70, No. 6, June 1981, pp. 9–14.
21. W. M. Ringle. "The America Who Remade 'Made in Japan.'" *Nation's Business*, Vol. 69, no. 2, 1981 , pp. 67–70.

Chapter 2. Why Has Purchasing Become So Important?

1. D. S. Ammer. "Materials Management as a Profit Center." *Harvard Business Review*, January-February 1969, pp. 72–82.
2. C. Babbage. *On the Economy of Machinery and Manufactures*, 2d. ed. London: Charles Knight, 1832.
3. R. J. Tersine and J. H. Campbell. *Modern Materials Management*. New York: North-Holland, 1977.
4. J. V. Centamore and R. W. Baer. "A Materials Management Survey." *Journal of Purchasing*, Vol. 7, No. 1, 1971, pp. 9–32.
5. J. G. Miller and P. Gilmour. "Materials Managers: Who Needs Them?" *Harvard Business Review*, July-August 1979, pp. 143–153.
6. S. Dowst. "Stormy Economy Brings Payoff for MM Systems." *Purchasing*, Vol. 8, No. 9, February 24, 1976(a), pp. 59–61.
7. L. Lee, Jr. and D. W. Dobler. *Purchasing and Materials Management*, 2d ed. New York: McGraw-Hill Book Company, 1971.
8. G. W. Aljian. *Purchasing Handbook*, 3d ed. New York: McGraw-Hill Book Company, 1973.
9. G. V. Schultz. "The Real Lowdown on Materials Management." *Factory*, December 1967, p. 49.
10. S. H. Rich. "The Impact of Materials Shortages on Purchasing Organization." *Journal of Purchasing*, Vol. 11, No. 1, 1975, pp. 13–17.
11. E. H. Bonfield and T. W. Speh. "Dimensions of Purchasing's Role in Industry." *Journal of Purchasing and Materials Management*, Vol. 13, No. 2, Summer 1977, pp. 10–17.
12. P. Baily and D. Farmer. *Purchasing Principles and Techniques*, 3d ed. London: Pitman Publishing Limited, 1977.
13. "Battling Inflation: The View from the Trenches." *Purchasing*, Vol. 24, No. 2, January 25, 1978, pp. 45–48.
14. N. Gaither. "The Effects of Inflation and Fuel Scarcity Upon Inventory Policies." *Production and Inventory Management*, Vol. 22, No. 2, 1981, pp. 37–48.

15. B. J. Lalonde and D. M. Lambert. "Management of Purchasing in an Uncertain Economy." *Journal of Purchasing and Materials Management*, Vol. 11, No. 4, Winter 1975, pp. 3–8.

16. "Purchasing Weighs Supply and Demand." *Purchasing*, Vol. 8, No. 12, June 22, 1976, pp. 73–75.

17. D. A. Kudrna. *Purchasing Manager's Decision*. Boston: Chaners Publishing Company Inc., 1975.

18. O. W. Wight. *MRP II: Unlocking America's Productivity Potential*. Boston: CBI Publishing Company, Inc., 1981.

19. "Delivery Performance Slips a Bit." *Purchasing*, Vol. 80, No. 9, May 11, 1976, p. 29.

20. C. J. Grayson, Jr. "Productivity in the United States." In J. E. Ross and W. C. Ross, *Japanese Quality Circles and Productivity*. New York: Reston Publishing Company, Inc., 1982, pp. 45–60.

21. B. B. Tregoe. "Productivity in America: Where It Went and How to Get It Back." *Management Review*, Vol. 72, No. 2, February 1983, pp. 23–45.

Chapter 3. How Is Traditional Purchasing Different from JIT Purchasing?

1. Y. Monden. "What Makes the Toyota Production System Really Tick?" *Industrial Engineering*, Vol. 13, No. 1, January 1981, pp. 36–40.

2. E. W. Deming. "Improvement of Quality and Productivity Through Action by Management." *National Productivity Review*, Winter 1981, pp. 12–14.

3. J. McElroy. "Making Just-In-Time Production Pay Off." *Automotive Industries*, Vol. 162, No. 2, February 1982, pp. 77–80.

4. W. B. England, *Procurement*, 4th ed. Homewood, Ill.: Richard D. Irwin, Inc., 1962.

5. "CEOs to Purchasing: Buy Quality, Staying Power." *Purchasing*, Vol. 94, No. 2, January 27, 1983, pp. 57–63.

6. G. W. Aljian. *Purchasing Handbook*, 3d ed. New York: McGraw-Hill Book Company, 1973.

7. G. W. Dickson. "An Analysis of Vendor Selection Systems and Decisions." *Journal of Purchasing*, Vol. 2, No. 1, 1966, p. 10.

8. R. J. Schonberger and A. Ansari. "Just-In-Time Purchasing Can Improve Quality," *Journal of Purchasing and Materials Management*, Vol. 20, No. 1, 1984, pp. 2–7.

9. B. B. Tregoe. "Productivity in America: Where It Went and How to Get It Back." *Management Review*, Vol. 72, No. 2, February 1983, pp. 23–45.

10. T. F. Dillion. "Inbound Routing Guides Make Sense, Save Dollars." *Purchasing*, Vol. 89, No. 7, October 9, 1980, pp. 67–70.

11. B. H. Berry. "Detroit Automakers Slim Down Inventory to Beef Up Profits." *Iron Age*, Vol. 225, No. 24, 1982, pp. 61–65.

12. D. S. Ammer. *Materials Management and Purchasing*. Homewood, Ill.: Richard D. Irwin, Inc., 1980.

Chapter 4. What Are the Benefits of JIT Purchasing?

1. A. Ansari and B. Modarress. "The Potential Benefits of Just-In-Time Purchasing for U.S Manufacturing." *Production and Inventory Management*, Vol. 28, No. 2, 1987, pp. 30–36.

Chapter 5. How Is JIT Purchasing Implemented?

1. C. R. Waters. "Why Everybody's Talking About Just-In-Time." *Inc*, Vol. 6, No. 3, March 1984, pp. 77–90.
2. A. Ansari. "Survey Identifies Critical Factors in Successful Implementation of Just-In-Time Purchasing Techniques." *Industrial Engineering*, Vol. 18, No. 10, 1986, pp. 44–50.
3. F. J. Quinn and L. H. Harrington. "How to Gain the JIT Advantage." *Traffic Management*, February 1987, pp. 39–52.
4. K. A. Wantuck. *Just-In-Time for America*. The Forum LTD, Milwaukee, Wisconsin, 1989.

Chapter 6. What Problems Are Encountered?

1. A. Ansari and B. Modarress. "Just-In-Time Purchasing: Problems and Solutions." *Journal of Purchasing and Materials Management*, Vol. 22, No. 2, 1986, pp. 11–15.
2. J. P. Kelleher. "A Comparison of Commercial and Defense Manufacturing." *APICS 31st Annual International Conference Proceedings*, October 17–21, 1988, Las Vegas, Nevada, pp. 733–736.
3. S. M. Horonec and G. Chassang. "Cost Management Steps Into the Future." A publication of Arthur Andersen and Company, Chicago, Illinois.

Chapter 7. How Are Freight Costs Reduced Under JIT Purchasing?

1. J. M. Masters. "The Effect of Consolidation on Customer Service," *Journal of Business Logistics*, Vol. 2, No. 1, 1980, pp. 55–74.
2. G. C. Jackson. "Evaluating Order Consolidation Strategies Using Simulation." *Journal of Business Logistics*, Vol. 2, No. 2, 1981, pp. 110–138.
3. M. C. Cooper. "Freight Consolidation and Warehouse Location Strategies in Physical Distribution Systems." *Journal of Business Logistics*, Vol. 4, No. 2, 1983, pp. 53–74.
4. A. Ansari and J. Heckle. "JIT Purchasing: Impact of Freight and Inventory Costs." *Journal of Purchasing and Materials Management*, Vol. 23, no. 2, 1987, pp. 24–28.

Chapter 8. What Transportation System Facilitates JIT Purchasing?

1. C. R. O'Neal. "The Buyer-Seller Linkage in a Just-In-Time Environment." *Journal of Purchasing and Materials Management*, Vol. 23, No. 1, 1987, pp. 7–13.
2. F. J. Quinn and L. H. Harrington. "How to Make Just-In-Time Work for You." *Traffic Management*, February 1987, pp. 40–52.
3. A. Ansari. "Survey Identifies Critical Factors in Successful Implementation of Just-In-Time Purchasing Techniques." *Industrial Engineering*, Vol. 18, No. 10, October 1986, pp. 44–50.
4. F. J. Quinn and L. H. Harrington. "How to Gain the JIT Advantage." *Traffic Management*, February 1987, p. 39.
5. R. C. Lieb and R. A. Miller. "JIT and Corporate Transportation Requirements," *Transportation Journal*, Vol. 27, No. 3, Spring 1988, pp. 5–10.

6. "How Important is Freight to Purchasing Departments?" *Purchasing*, Vol. 94, No. 7, April 14, 1983, pp. 41–51.
7. W. J. Cook. "Truck 54, Where Are You?" *U.S. News & World Report*, March 21, 1988, p. 64.

Chapter 9. How Does JIT Purchasing Improve Product Quality and Productivity?

1. D. S. Ammer. "Materials Management as a Profit Center," *Harvard Business Review*, January-February 1969, pp. 72–82.
2. P. Baily and D. Farmer. *Purchasing Principles and Techniques*, 3d ed. London: Pitman Publishing Limited, 1977.
3. P. B. Crosby. "A Look at the Japanese and American Styles of Management of Quality and Productivity." *Quality*, Vol. 19, No. 6, June 1980, pp. 36–37.
4. A. Ansari and B. Modarress. "JIT Purchasing as a Quality and Productivity Center." *International Journal of Production Research*, Vol. 26, No. 1, 1988, pp. 19–26.
5. C. R. O'Neal. "The Buyer-Seller Linkage in a Just-In-Time Environment." *Journal of Purchasing and Materials Management*, Spring 1987, pp. 7–13.

Chapter 10. What Is the Role of Quality Control in JIT Purchasing?

1. G. Taguchi. "Off-Line and On-Line Quality Control Systems." Presented at the International Conference on Quality Control, 1978, Tokyo.
2. Quality Engineering Using Design of Experiments, *Third Supplier Symposium on Taguchi Methods*. American Supplier Institute, Dearborn, MI, October 8–9, 1985.
3. W. A. Shewhart. *Economic Control of Quality of Management Products*. New York: D. Van Nostrand Company, Inc., 1931.
4. E. W. Deming. *Quality and Productivity and Competitive Position*. Cambridge, Mass.: Massachusetts Institute of Technology, 1982.
5. B. Modarress and A. Ansari. "Quality Control Techniques in U.S. Firms: A Survey." *Production and Inventory Management*, Vol. 30, No. 2, 1989, pp. 58–62.
6. K. Ishikawa. *What Is Total Quality Control*. Englewood Cliffs, N.J.: Prentice-Hall, Inc., 1985.

Chapter 11. What Is the Impact of QC Techniques and JIT on Quality Cost?

1. D. Bain. *The Productivity Prescription*. New York: McGraw-Hill, 1982.
2. E. W. Deming. *Statistical Adjustment of Data*. New York: John Wiley and Sons, 1943.
3. R. J. Schonberger. *Japanese Manufacturing Techniques: Nine Hidden Lessons in Simplicity*. New York: The Free Press, 1982.
4. J. M. Juran. *Quality Control Handbook*. New York: McGraw-Hill Book Company, 1974.
5. W. J. Morse. "Measuring Quality Costs." *Cost and Management*, July-August 1983, pp. 16–20.

6. J. Main. "The Battle for Quality Begins." *Fortune,* December 29, 1980, pp. 28–33.

7. *Quality Management and Engineering Magazine.* Editorial. Vol. 12, No. 3, 1983, p. 11.

8. H. G. Gilmore. "Consumer Product Quality Control and Cost Revisited." *Quality Progress,* April 1983, pp. 28–32.

9. P. B. Crosby. "A Look at the Japanese and American Styles of Management of Quality and Productivity." *Quality,* Vol. 19, No. 6, June 1980, pp. 36–37.

10. J. McElroy. "Making Just-In-Time Production Pay Off." *Automotive Industries,* Vol. 162, No. 2, 1982, pp. 77–80.

11. G. Taguchi. *On-Line Quality Control During Production.* Tokyo: Japanese Standards Association, 1981.

12. J. M. Juran. "Product Quality—A Prescription for the West." *Control and Applied Statistics,* Vol. 27, No. 9, 1982, pp. 719–720.

13. E. W. Deming. "Improvement of Quality and Productivity Through Action by Management." *National Productivity Review,* Winter 1981, pp. 12–14.

14. S. Shingo. *Study of Toyota Production System from Industrial Engineering Viewpoint.* Tokyo: Japan Management Association, 1981.

Index